MW00874766

Love That Heals

Healing the Sin-Sick Soul

By
Pastor Bill Chambers

Edited by Floyd Phillips

About the Author:

Bill Chambers is a retired Adventist pastor. You contact him via
the following:

By mail: **By phone:** 770 530-2308
Bill Chambers
115 Lazarus Dr   **By email:** wrchambers@att.net
Hiram, Ga 30141

Table of Contents

3

Before you begin…

Before his downfall a man's heart is proud, but humility comes before honor. He who answers before listening-- that is his folly and his shame.

Proverbs 18:12-13

This is not a book written to entertain, but for study. It is written with the hope that the reader will approach the message contained within with a humble spirit and an open mind. According to the text from Proverbs above it is a foolish thing to be close-minded. God only knows how many people have forfeited beneficial knowledge and comfort to their souls because they would not read or listen to someone that is not of their particular church denomination or because they had heard some negative report about them from someone else. Even if you do not initially agree with what you read in these pages, I hope you will at least be provoked to search the scriptures to prove whether or not these things are true.

At the time of the completing of this book, I am seventy plus years old. I have had many and various experiences in life, but none of which has been more rewarding and fulfilling than the study of God's Word and learning more about His gracious ways and His great desire to save His wayward children.

I am not a Theologian, Bible scholar, or Seminary Professor. I do not have a MA, BA, MDIV, or PhD. But I have spent untold hours reading, studying, and meditating upon the Holy Scriptures as well as a wide range of works of those who are qualified to call themselves theologians, Bible scholars, and professors.

I have found by both study and personal experience that God meets us where we are and leads us no faster than we are able to follow. The Bible teaches that the Christian must never become stagnant, but is to be continually seeking, learning, and to *"grow in the grace and knowledge of our Lord and Savior Jesus Christ."*[1] But each person must be allowed to grow at his or her own pace.

Being close minded myself some years ago, I am not sure that the message contained in this book is one that I may have been willing to accept at one time. Therefore I realize that some who read this book may not be ready for its message either. Having said that, I also want to point out that the message of salvation in this book is not intended to deny any other creditable way of understanding this critical subject, but rather to show what I believe is a more comprehensive model of God's wonderful plan to save and restore His children. And more than that, I hope that the

---

1 - 2 Peter 3:18

reader will see God in a new way that will bring a real peace and joy into their heart and life. I have attempted to put into my own words a way of understanding the science and experience of salvation that is logical and clear and most important, biblical. I have attempted to write this book in such a way that any person who can read will be able to comprehend its message. It is in this spirit that I present this work for your consideration.

Chapter One

Dark Speech

But this is not true of my servant Moses; he is faithful in all my house. With him I speak face to face, clearly and not in riddles; he sees the form of the LORD.

Numbers 12: 7-8

Once an old farmer was attending a board meeting in the little country church where he had been a member most of his life. During the meeting the pastor brought up the suggestion that the church purchase a chandelier for their sanctuary. The old farmer was quick to respond. He stood up and said "Preacher, I know you mean well, but I'm agin it; first of all, we ain't got nobody who knows how to play one of them thangs, and besides that, what we really need is more lights in here!"

This story is told as a joke, but one of the things that make it so laughable is that we all know it really could have happened just as described. Many people in our "enlightened age," because of simple ignorance are left in the dark. The reason for much of this, especially in the area of religion, is the misunderstanding of words and terms used by people who may not even know the meaning themselves.

There is a lot of what I refer to as "dark speech" in the Christian Church today. By the term "dark speech," I mean words and expressions in which the definitions are not really known, or that are difficult to comprehend or understand. The Christian "clichés" and "theological" words and terms that we sometimes hear, and may even repeat but often don't really know what they mean. This kind of "dark speech" is heard in sermons and religious classes; it is found in the songs of church hymnals and read in our Christian literature. It has become commonplace and the average Christian has become so accustomed to it that most are unaware of its existence. You, dear reader, may be unaware of it. But I hope this will not be the case after you have read this chapter.

Jesus, speaking to the Jews who were seeking to kill Him because He claimed that He was the Son of God, said *"You diligently study the Scriptures because you think that by them you possess eternal life. These are the Scriptures that testify about me, yet you refuse to come to me to have life."*[1]

Jesus was implying that it is possible for a person to search and study the scriptures and still not know God. When the Bible uses the word *"know"* in this way it means

---

1 - John 5:39-40

more than simply being introduced to, or knowing information "about" someone; it implies a close, intimate relationship with them; a relationship like that of close friends, or a husband and wife who truly love and honor one another. Christians in this age that well may culminate with the second coming of Christ, especially need to **know** God intellectually and spiritually, personally and intimately as a close Friend.

If we aren't studying the Bible to better know God, chances are we may be doing it for the wrong reason! But the point I want to make in this chapter is this – if in our study of the Bible, due to misinterpretation, poor translation or misunderstanding, ("dark speech"), if it does not reveal to us the truth about God, but rather contributes to the development or reinforcement of wrong understandings of Him, we could find ourselves in the same place spiritually as the Jews Jesus was speaking to long ago.

Communication is critical in relationships, especially intimate ones. Exodus tells us *"The LORD would speak to Moses face to face, as a man speaks with his friend."*[2] We can learn how God speaks to His friends by examining how God spoke to Moses – *"With him* (Moses) *will I speak mouth to mouth, even apparently, and*

---

2 - Exodus 33:11

not in dark speeches; and the similitude of the LORD shall he behold:"[3]

First, this verse says God spoke to Moses *"mouth to mouth,"* that is, with no one in between Him and Moses. This was demonstrated when God called Moses up on Mt. Sinai to receive the Ten Commandments: *"When the people saw the thunder and lightning and heard the trumpet and saw the mountain in smoke, they trembled with fear. They stayed at a distance and said to Moses, 'Speak to us yourself and we will listen. But do not have God speak to us or we will die.' Moses said to the people, 'Do not be afraid. God has come to test you, so that the fear of God will be with you to keep you from sinning.' The people remained at a distance, while Moses approached the thick darkness where God was."*[4]

The people *"remained at a distance"* because they were afraid of God, but Moses, because of his personal relationship with God knew that there was no reason to be afraid. Some Christians have been taught that we must have a "go between," a rabbi, priest or some other "holy" person between us and God. Yet in reality, if we are in right relationship with God we need no one between us and Him.

---

3   - Numbers 12:8 KJV
4   - Exodus 20:18

Notice there was no one between God and Moses when he went up on the mount!

Once we learn the truth about God, like Moses, we will know there is absolutely no reason to be afraid of our heavenly Father. Jesus Christ, who is God in the flesh, in coming to this world means that God himself came to be our intermediary. We could not go up to heaven to find God, so He came down to find us! How kind of Him to do that.

Back to our text in Numbers 12. Now that we understand the term *"mouth to mouth,"* what does the next phrase, *"even apparently"* mean? It is from a Hebrew word meaning *"clearly"* and is immediately followed by *"not in dark speeches."* This passage tells us that God prefers to speak to His friends like Moses, clearly, not in puzzles or riddles or symbolic, figurative language. God wants that kind of relationship with His people yet today, and as we noted earlier Jesus came to help us with that.

The Lord considers His followers His friends and He does not want them in the dark, misunderstanding and ignorant of the truth. Jesus said *"I no longer call you servants, because a servant does not know his master's business. Instead, I have called you friends, for everything that I learned from my Father I have made known to you."[5]*

Did you catch that last part? *"I have called you friends, for everything that I learned from my Father I have made known to you."* The problem was then, as it still is today, that a lot of what Jesus said to the disciples was not comprehended because of traditional beliefs taught by religious leaders whom they saw as authorities not to be questioned. Many things Jesus said to the disciples seemed like strange talk to them; that is why Jesus said what He did in the following passage:

"Though I have been speaking figuratively, a time is coming when I will no longer use this kind of language but will tell you plainly about my Father. In that day you will ask in my name. I am not saying that I will ask the Father on your behalf. No, the Father himself loves you because you have loved me and have believed that I came from God. I came from the Father and entered the world; now I am leaving the world and going back to the Father." Then Jesus' disciples said, "Now you are speaking clearly and without figures of speech."[6]

---

5 - John 15:15
6 - John 16:25-29

12

Here, even though Jesus spoke to the disciples plainly, they still didn't understand everything He wanted them to know. But the day would come when they would no longer need types and figures, parables or symbols. The day would come when they would understand the truth about God the Father, and the things Jesus had told them would become clear and no longer sound like *"dark speech."* That day finally came for them after Christ's resurrection and the outpouring of the Holy Spirit on the day of Pentecost.

But what about us? Do we hear a lot of *"dark speech"* today in the Church? What about the Christian *"clichés"* we hear? Terms like *"Covered by the blood"* or *"Praying in the spirit"* or *"Righteousness by faith."* These are precious phrases that have been used by many Christians for years. We sing them from the hymnals and hear the preachers use them, yet many of them can't be found in the Bible. I would dare say that very few of us have a good understanding of what many of these phrases really mean.

Then there are the words like *"propitiation,"* *"justification,"* *"sanctification."* These are found in the Bible and we hear them read often, yet few of us know their true meaning. Many books have been written on

13

"justification" and *"sanctification,"* often only making them seem more complicated than before. They seem like just more *"dark speech."*

Adding to this problem, over the years many of the words used in the widely accepted King James Version Bible have become antiquated, or outdated. For example the word "wist" commonly used in England in 1611 has long since been replaced with the word "know." Some words mean exactly the opposite of what they did when the KJV translation was first completed. For example the term "by and by" in the KJV was translated from the Greek word "eutheos" which means "immediately" or "at once." That was the meaning of the term "by and by" in England in 1611. But today "by and by" means just the opposite. Today it means, not immediately, but sometime later.

Another example is the word "atonement." The origin of this word goes back to the 1400's when it originally meant, "to unite," "to reconcile," literally "to be at one," thus at-one-ment or atonement. But in the 1600's the word came to be understood as "appeasement," or to use the Latin word we find in most Bibles, "propitiation." (The word "propitiation" is translated from a Greek word which literally means "mercy seat.") Today in modern dictionaries the original definition of atonement which was

14

"reconciliation" is listed as obsolete and in its place is given the definition – "to atone for" or "to appease."

An example of the use of the word atonement as we understand it today would be something like this: If I forget my wife's birthday, then I must do something special, like bring her a dozen roses to make "atonement" or to "atone" for my shortcoming in forgetting her birthday. I must "appease" her, so she will not be angry with me anymore and forgive me.

Because of this change in the meaning of the word atonement from its original meaning, many believe Christ's death on the cross was to "atone" or "appease" God's anger so we can be forgiven and brought back into His good graces again. This can have serious spiritual implications with many Christians seeing the Atonement of Christ in a way that reflects badly on the character of God which we will discuss in detail in another chapter.

Since the Scriptures were originally written in Hebrew and Greek, we can see how the use of words that accurately reflect the original words is critical for the reader to better understand what the prophets intended to say. Some modern translations have done this to some extent. For example, some now use "set right" in place of "justification" and "keep right" instead of "sanctification," and "reconciliation" or "atonement" instead of "propitiation." These terms more correctly reflect the meaning of the original words and are certainly easier for us to understand.

I believe when people hear certain terms and words but do not know what they mean, believing that a good Christian should know the meanings they are ashamed to ask, *"What does that mean?"* But remember, Jesus said that to enter into the kingdom we must *"become as little children,"* that is, being humble, teachable, questioning, and eager to learn. So don't be afraid to ask questions!

A gifted speaker once wrote – *"A little girl once asked me, 'Are you going to speak this afternoon?' 'No, not this afternoon,' I replied. 'I am very sorry,' she said. 'I thought you were going to speak, and I asked several of my friends to come. Will you please ask the minister to speak easy words that we can understand? Will you please tell him that we do not understand large words, like 'justification' and 'sanctification'? We do not know what these words mean.'"*[7]

The little girl's complaint contains a lesson worthy of consideration. There are many who would do well to heed the request, *"speak easy words that we may know*

---

7 - Counsels to Parents, Teachers, and Students, page 254, 1913

what you mean." Teachers and preachers should follow the example of Jesus who taught so simply that all, even the children, could understand!

The prophet Amos says the day will come when *"Men will stagger from sea to sea and wander from north to east, searching for the word of the LORD, but they will not find it."*[8] Some people believe when the anti-Christ comes he will have the authorities take away all our Bibles as the medieval church did back in the dark ages. But think of what an impossible task that would be today! No, the authorities are not going to come and take our Bibles away, but there are multitudes of people who will not study for themselves and at best will only listen to what preachers and teachers have to say. When those preachers and teachers speak with a lot of *"dark speech"* and people do not ask, *"What does that mean?"* or will not put forth an effort to learn the meaning for themselves, they will not <u>know</u> the Word of the Lord. Thus, in a sense the Word is taken away from them even while they hold the Bible in their hand!

We must know the Word and be careful to confirm from the Word, the teachings of others. Note carefully these words written long ago:

---

8 - Amos 8:12

"Christ had many truths to give to His disciples, of which He could not speak, because they did not advance with the light that was flashed upon the Levitical laws and the sacrificial offerings. They did not embrace the light, advance with the light, and follow on to still greater brightness as Providence should lead the way. And for the same reason Christ's disciples of today do not comprehend important matters of truth. So dull has been the comprehension of even those who teach the truth to others that many things cannot be opened to them until they reach heaven. It ought not to be so. They close their minds as though there were no more for them to learn, and should the Lord attempt to lead them on, they would not take up with the increased light. The development of truth will be the reward to the humble-hearted seeker, who will fear God and walk with Him."[9]

The good news is that you and I have a choice. We can have the attitude of an unquestioning servant and cling to the dark speech while murmuring and complaining, *"I don't know why you want me to do that Lord... I don't understand...but I guess for the servant it's not to know the reason why, but to do or die."*

_____

9 - Vol. 16 MR No. 1201

On the other hand, like Moses, we can choose to be God's friend and ask, *"Lord I really want to understand – is that really what you said? And Lord, what did you mean when you said that?"* Jesus has assured us that if we ask *"it will be given to you; seek and you will find."*[10]

With all the tools for Bible study available to us today, the commentaries, Hebrew and Greek dictionaries, various Bible versions and easy to use computer programs, there is no excuse for us to remain in the dark about "dark speech." Let us strive for the deeper understanding we need. It is especially important that we have a clearer picture of our Heavenly Father and His character which Jesus has gone to such great lengths to show us through His life and death as recorded in the Scriptures. In the next chapter we will discuss why it is so critical that we have the right picture or understanding of God's character.

---

10 - Matthew 7:7

Chapter Two

Our Picture of God and Why It is Important

Now this is eternal life: that they may know you, the only true God, and Jesus Christ, whom you have sent.

John 17:3

A critically important doctrine for the Church, especially in these last days, is the truth about the character of God. This is important for two reasons.

First – Knowing the truth about God's character will safeguard us from the unintentional worship of false Christs. The Bible says *"For false Christs and false prophets will appear and perform great signs and miracles to deceive even the elect-- if that were possible."[11]*

Many believe that one day near the end of time, in addition to an anti-Christ appearing as some charismatic, powerful human being who will openly oppose God and rule the world, that Satan himself will appear "in the flesh" so to speak, claiming to be Christ. In fact, the word "anti-Christ" in the biblical Greek is "antee-Christos" which means "in place of Christ." It seems probable that Satan will come claiming to be Christ, "in place of" Christ, thus making Satan himself the genuine anti-Christ!

---

11 - Matthew 24:24

Satan, having superhuman powers, will be able to *"perform great signs and miracles"[12]* the likes of which the world has never seen and the majority of people in the world will believe that he is Christ as he claims; believing that the miraculous things he is able to perform can only come from Divine power. So no matter who comes before that, even someone who appears to be a great leader and may apparently unite the world as the anti-Christ is expected to do – ultimately in the end Satan will be the one who *"sets himself up in God's temple, proclaiming himself to be God."[13]* Satan is the original and ultimate anti-Christ!

One point we need to be clear on is that great demonstrations of power and miracles cannot always be trusted as coming from God. Satan can also perform great signs and wonders. But what may be more dangerous is that with his superhuman intelligence he can twist the Scriptures with such subtle deception that he can easily deceive millions into believing they have the truth when they actually are embracing a lie. But – and this is important to remember – although Satan can deceive with miracles and words, he cannot perfectly impersonate God's character of unselfish, unconditional love! That is the very

---

12 - Matthew 24:24
13 - 2 Thessalonians 2:4

thing that will give Satan away to those who truly know God well. Therefore, only the knowledge of God's true character can be trusted in the last days to distinguish the true Christ from the false and enable one to recognize the impostor!

Second – And this is equally an important reason – knowing the truth about God's character will always have an enormous effect on our own character. The Bible says in Psalms 135 –

"The idols of the nations are silver and gold, made by the hands of men. They have mouths, but cannot speak, eyes, but they cannot see; they have ears, but cannot hear, nor is there breath in their mouths. Those who make them will be like them, and so will all who trust in them."[14]

Did you catch the point of this passage? Those who make the idols, and those who trust in the idols, will become <u>like</u> the idols! This does not mean that a person will become a statue of brass or granite as those idols were, but it means that the person who worships the idol will develop a character like the character that the god that the idol or statue represents is believed to have.

---

14 - Psalms 135:15-18

There is a natural and spiritual law that says, "By beholding we will become changed into the same image." That is, a person will begin to copy and eventually develop the character and perceived values of the idol, the celebrity, or god they revere and worship. This is known as the "Law of Worship."

An example of this human trait is seen in the way many people relate to popular movie or rock stars, which ironically are often referred to as "idols." As people become devoted fans of these celebrities many begin to dress like them, talk like them, adopting their same values attempting to emulate them in every way possible.

This same principle applies to the worship of God as well. Note the following - *"But we all, with open face beholding as in a glass the glory of the Lord, are changed into the same image from glory to glory, even as by the Spirit of the Lord."[15]*

This verse is saying that by beholding the glory of the Lord a person is changed into the same image by the work of the Holy Spirit. *"Beholding"* means to observe, to contemplate, to meditate upon. In this case a person beholding the Lord would not become omnipotent (all

---

15 - 2 Corinthians 3:18 KJV

powerful), omniscient (all knowing), and omnipresent (everywhere at once) as God is, but they would begin to develop the same nature or character as the Lord. They would truly come to be more like Jesus!

You will notice the text says that by *"beholding the glory of the Lord."* What is this "glory" of the Lord that this verse refers to? If we go back to the story of Moses we find that he once asked the Lord to show him His glory.

"Then Moses said, 'Now show me your glory.' And the LORD said, 'I will cause all my goodness to pass in front of you, and I will proclaim my name, the LORD, in your presence.'"[16]

Notice when Moses asked to see His glory, the Lord said *"I will cause all my goodness to pass in front of you."* The Lord put Moses in the cleft of the rock and then the Bible says –

And he passed in front of Moses, proclaiming, "The LORD, the LORD, the compassionate and gracious God, slow to anger, abounding in love and faithfulness, maintaining love to thousands, and forgiving wickedness, rebellion and sin...."[17]

---

16 - Exodus 33:18-19
17 - Exodus 34:6-7

The glory of the Lord that God wanted Moses to see was not His form and awesome power but rather the *"glory"* of His gracious character! His gracious character is what He wants us to behold today that we may be changed into His image and that we may become more like Him.

For example, because of our selfish human nature, we would not naturally think of loving our enemies. The human nature compels us to hate our enemy. But as we study the Bible we read that Jesus says we are to forgive and love our enemies. But more than just telling us what we should do, He demonstrated it. When we see Christ forgive and love His enemies, even die for them, it awakens something inside of us that empowers us to also love our enemies too! That *something* is implanted by God in each heart to respond to this very stimulation. Jesus is our model of true righteousness. If we are going to idolize a man, it should be the *"Man Jesus Christ"*[18] who, being *"the exact representation of his being,"*[19] is the perfect representation of the character of God Himself.

So we have two distinct choices before us. One is to behold some worldly idol, person, or system, and as a result become worldly, or we can behold Jesus and become like

---

18 - 1 Timothy 2:5
19 - Hebrews 1:3

Him! However, if because of misunderstanding or false teaching we have a false picture of God, we will in a sense then worship a false god. One thoughtful Bible commentator made the following insightful statement:

"Multitudes have a wrong conception of God and his attributes, and are as truly serving a false god as were the worshipers of Baal."[20]

Does this statement help you to see why our picture of God is so important? What makes the worship of a false god so dangerous is that we increasingly reflect the character of the god we worship. In the case of the professed Christian, if we view our Heavenly Father as arbitrary, rigid, harsh, angry with sinners, condemning of them and needing to be appeased, then we will likely become rigid, harsh Christians who judge and condemn others whom we view as sinners, overlooking the fact that we may be a greater sinner in our judging and condemning them! You may recall that Jesus said –

"They will put you out of the synagogue; in fact, a time is coming when anyone who kills you will think he is offering a service to God."[21]

---

20 - Review and Herald, Nov. 6, 1913

Note, these are religious people doing these things thinking it to be a service to God! Then in verse 3 Jesus tells us why they do this – *"They will do such things because they have not known the Father or me."*

They do this because of their misunderstanding of God's nature, believing He would approve of such conduct! They believe that they are simply His instruments to carry out His will. Does the church today see God in this light? Is He seen as an executioner of the wicked? If so, what effect will that perception have on our character and how we look at those whom we see as hopeless sinners? Keep this question in mind as we continue our study.

So how do we know we are beholding the true God and not some distorted, false image? How do we know we have a right picture of God? We do that by laying aside our pride, our preconceived ideas and opinions and go to God's Word *"as little children"* with an open, inquisitive mind.

As we go through the Bible we find different pictures of God. We see a God who drowned the world in the flood; a God who came down in fire and flame and thundered on Mt. Sinai; a God who consumed Nadab and Abihu with fire; a God who ordered the stoning of Achan and his family and rained fire down from heaven on Mt.

Carmel. We see a fearful picture of an awesome deity not to be trifled with.

But before we draw any hasty conclusions we need to look at **all** the Bible says about God and then think some things through. Do you think God relished doing those terrible things we read about Him doing in the Old Testament? Parents, do you enjoy disciplining your children, especially when it requires punishment? But which shows the greater love, to refuse to discipline the child because you are afraid the child will come to dislike you, or run the risk of being thought badly of in order to properly train the child for his own good? The Lord is not willing to let his children perish uninstructed and unwarned, so He ran the risk of intervening in the lives of men and women. Of course Satan has taken advantage of that to make God look like a cruel tyrant.

There is a danger of the Bible reader becoming preoccupied with fearful pictures of God in scripture and overlooking the other pictures that are there. While it is true there can be seen a God of wrath, there can also be seen the picture of God as a loving Father who is unbelievably patient with His disobedient and rebellious children. We can see a loving God who blesses and provides for the just and the unjust – the good and the evil.

There is no denying the contrasts that are found in the Bible. But are we to accept the ones we like and disregard the rest? No, that would be dishonesty with the Scriptures. The key is to find the greater reality behind these two contrasting pictures to discover the real truth.

For example, if you had a medical book that had only the pictures and descriptions of the deadly effects of disease in it, that would not be very helpful but rather it would likely be very frightening. On the other hand, if that medical book had not only pictures and descriptions of the effects of disease, but also the treatments and cures for those diseases, then it would be a very helpful book.

In the same way, if we only look at the pictures of God in the Bible that show Him exercising wrath and vengeance in certain situations, we may view him as a harsh and wrathful God. But in the Bible we not only have the ugly record of sin and how God has had to deal with a rebellious, sinful people at times; we also have a record of a loving God who has demonstrated that He has forgiven sin and is working patiently and compassionately to reach and save everyone He can. This makes the Bible the good book that ultimately reveals and vindicates the character of God.

Nevertheless, there are still those who see two different Gods in the Bible and thus in their minds they divide the Trinity against itself. First they see the God of the Old Testament as "the Father": severe, arbitrary, wrathful, and unforgiving. Then they see God's Son, Jesus in the New Testament as gentle and merciful, kind and compassionate, not at all like the Father. They have been told the Son must plead with the Father and even sacrifice His life in order for the Father to forgive, as though the Father were reluctant to pardon the sinner, demanding retribution for His broken law.

However, there is a problem with this view when we consider that Jesus plainly stated, "*I and the Father are one.*"[22] Any teaching that portrays the Father and Son as not being in total, complete harmony and union with one another separates the Trinity and is erroneous. These kinds of errors cloud our pictures of God. (We will take a closer look at the Trinity in the next chapter.)

It is sad that there are religions today that, while claiming to believe in God do not accept the truth that Jesus is God. The tragedy of that is that in rejecting this truth they are left with no accurate picture of God. But the Bible gives us a perfect photograph of God, and that is Jesus Christ who came to reveal what the Father, so often misunderstood and lied about, is really like. That is the

---

22 - John 10:30

reason God didn't send an angel, for an angel simply could not fully and perfectly portray the character of God. Only God could do that, so He came Himself in His Son.

Without Jesus it might be impossible to know what God is really like and we would have no Divine Model to pattern our lives after. Without the true picture of God as seen in Christ, men will develop a false picture of God and thus be worshiping a false god. As I mentioned earlier, by worshiping a false god they will become like that false god rather than becoming like Jesus. I believe this is one reason for the long history of violence we witness in many religions, even with Christianity. It is the reason for the continuing violence we see today by those who claim to be believers in God. Just consider the picture of God that terrorists and extremists must have. They believe in a god who will cut your hand off if you steal, hang you if you commit adultery, behead you if you reject his prophet! But on the other hand, if everyone saw God as being just like Jesus they would find no place for violence against another, even against their enemies.

I remember seeing a sign hanging in a church classroom years ago that said "Don't get your facts from the snake!" Good Advice! We must be careful we aren't getting our information from the snake, Satan. Satan lied about God to the angels in heaven; he lied about God in the Garden of Eden, and Satan has lied about God in the Church and Satan is continually misrepresenting the character of God to human minds and hearts.

Chapter Three

Understanding the Trinity

But the Counselor, the Holy Spirit, whom the Father will send in my name, will teach you all things and will remind you of everything I have said to you.

John 14:26

We have evidence for one God in three persons, commonly referred to as the "Trinity" because of verses like this one – *"But the Counselor, the Holy Spirit,* (one person) *whom the Father* (a second person) *will send in my name, will teach you all things, and will remind you of everything I* (Jesus, a third person) *have said to you."[1]*

It is easily seen here that there are three persons in this verse, the Holy Spirit, the Father, and the Son, Jesus. The three persons are co-eternal, co-divine, and co-equal, that is, they are all God, they all have existed from eternity and one does not have authority or rank over the other. They are in perfect harmony and unity of purpose and character with each other. As a matter of fact, anywhere you find the name "Father" or "Son" or "Holy Spirit" you can substitute the one title – "God."

God is infinite, limitless in power, time, and space. It is impossible for mankind with his limited mental

---

1 - John 14:26

abilities, to grasp all that God is. So to help His finite (limited) creatures better understand His divine nature and enter into relationship with Him, the three persons of the have taken upon themselves different roles.

One member of the Trinity has taken the role of the Father. The Father is understood as the Almighty God seated on the throne in heaven. He is the One who is in control, directing the affairs of the universe. The Father is the One who *"lives in unapproachable light,"*[2] the One who is all knowing and sees *"the end from the beginning."*[3] The Father is reigning from His position seated on the throne in Heaven twenty-four seven, continuously from eternity past to eternity future; He never leaves the throne.

At the same time the Bible teaches God is omnipresent. That means He is ever-present and everywhere, all the time. It is difficult for man with his limited knowledge to comprehend how God can be everywhere in the universe at the same time and still be seen as the One seated on the throne too. This is where another person of the Trinity comes in. He takes the role of the Spirit, the One who is understood as being everywhere and invisible. He is the Divine Helper, who instead of

---

2 - 1 Timothy 6:16
3 - Isaiah 46:10

sitting on the throne in heaven, sits on the throne of the hearts of believers, teaching, convicting and persuading on behalf of God.

Finally, men need a visual picture of God, to see *"God with flesh on"* so to speak; to see how God would live and behave if He were one of us. This is the role of the Son, the One who came *"in the flesh"* to give us a clearer picture of what God is really like. The Son in this role is also the Intermediary. As it says in 1 Timothy – *"There is one mediator* (intermediary) *between God and men, the man Christ Jesus."*[4]

Jesus is God in the flesh. That means that God in the person of Jesus Christ is our Intercessor. As previously stated, since it is impossible for us to go to heaven to find God, we need someone to bring God down to us, and Jesus Christ is the person of the Trinity who does that.

The Son is unique. He is *"Jacob's ladder,"* the link between heaven and earth, between God and man. And just as the person of the Father remains on the throne and the person of the Holy Spirit remains the Invisible Guide in the heart, so the person of the Son remains the Intermediary, the one and only link between heaven and earth. Either as a Man among us (Immanuel), or as our High Priest in the

---

4 - 1 Timothy 2:5

heavenly sanctuary,[5] He has been in this role from the beginning. Note the words of Paul in Colossians –

"He is the image of the invisible God, the firstborn over all creation. For by him all things were created: things in heaven and on earth, visible and invisible, whether thrones or powers or rulers or authorities; all things were created by him and for him. He is before all things, and in him all things hold together. And he is the head of the body, the church."[6]

In this passage notice that (1) He is the image of the invisible God – becoming One that could be seen; (2) He is the Creator as well as Savior; and (3) He is the Head of the Church. Jesus the Son is all of these.

He is the Lord God we read of in the Old Testament. His voice was the voice of God that spoke and the earth was created. His hands were the hands of God that formed man from the dust of the earth. He was the God who walked with Adam and Eve in the cool of the evening in the Garden of Eden. He was the God who appeared to Moses in the burning bush. He was *"the Angel of the Lord"* who led Israel through the wilderness in a pillar of cloud by day and

---

5   - Hebrews 8:1
6   - Colossians 1:15-18

a pillar of fire by night. He was the God who came down on Mt. Sinai in fire and flame and gave the commandments.

For clear evidence of this compare the previous text, *"For by him all things were created: things in heaven and on earth,"* with what we find in Nehemiah –

"You alone are the LORD. You made the heavens, even the highest heavens, and all their starry host, the earth and all that is on it, the seas and all that is in them. You give life to everything, and the multitudes of heaven worship you."[7]

Who is this speaking of? According to what we just read in Colossians, this is the Son of God. This is Christ before he came in the flesh as the man Jesus. Nehemiah continues in verse 7 –

"You are the LORD God, who chose Abram and brought him out of Ur of the Chaldeans and named him Abraham. You found his heart faithful to you, and you made a covenant with him to give to his descendants the land of the Canaanites, Hittites, Amorites, Perizzites, Jebusites and Girgashites. You have kept your promise because you are righteous. You saw the suffering of our forefathers in Egypt; you heard their cry at the Red Sea. You sent miraculous signs and wonders against Pharaoh, against all his

---

7   - Nehemiah 9:6

officials and all the people of his land, for you knew how arrogantly the Egyptians treated them. You made a name for yourself, which remains to this day. You divided the sea before them, so that they passed through it on dry ground, but you hurled their pursuers into the depths, like a stone into mighty waters. By day you led them with a pillar of cloud, and by night with a pillar of fire to give them light on the way they were to take. You came down on Mount Sinai; you spoke to them from heaven. You gave them regulations and laws that are just and right, and decrees and commands that are good."[8]

Again, who did all this? The same One who created all things in heaven and earth, the Son of God. Paul clearly states this –

"...and to make all see what is the fellowship of the mystery, which from the beginning of the ages has been hidden in God who created all things through Jesus Christ."[9]

"God who created all things through Jesus Christ." In the preceding texts it can be clearly seen that the Son, whom we best know as Jesus, was the Creator, the Lord

---

8   - Nehemiah 9:7-13
9   - Ephesians 3:9 NKJV

God and Redeemer in the Old Testament as well as the Lord and Savior in the New. The Son was the person of the Godhead who gave up His position equal with the Father on the throne in heaven. He was the One who suffered and struggled with the human race from creation. And when the time was right, He came and lived with men as a man, One they could see, touch and talk to. And He is the One who died the death of the cross and arose the third day. All this was the Father's plan, carried out by the Son, impressed on our hearts by the Spirit and witnessed by the angels.

The Trinity is one God. Jesus said, *"Anyone who has seen me has seen the Father."*[10] In other words, the Father is just like me! Then Jesus said, *"I will ask the Father, and he will give you another Counselor."*[11] The *"Counselor"* referred to here is the Holy Spirit. The word *"another"* is translated from the Greek word *"allos"* meaning, *"of the same kind."* In other words, Jesus is saying the Holy Spirit whom the Father will send to be your Counselor is just like Me! I am just like the Father and the Holy Spirit is just like Me. We are all the same; We are all One!

---

10 - John 14:9
11 - John 14:16

The words Jesus spoke are stunning when we truly comprehend what Jesus is saying when He said, *"Anyone who has seen me has seen the Father."*[12] In other words Jesus is saying, *"If you have seen me you have seen God! God is just like me!"* The Trinity cannot be separated. If the Father had come instead of the Son, it would have made no difference. God is just like Jesus! That is good news! <u>That</u> is the everlasting gospel! I hope this brief study has given you a little better understanding of the Trinity.

In spite of all the Bible teaches, I believe that far too many Christians today have an unbiblical, distorted picture of God. And one thing I feel is largely responsible for this is the traditional teaching of the plan of salvation which is modeled after the legal, law-oriented court system of the Western World. In the following chapter we will begin to look at this traditional model of salvation, and how that through distorted and unbiblical teachings many have a false conception of the character of God, the nature of sin, why Jesus had to die and how we are saved.

---

12 - John 14:9

Chapter Four

Examining the Legal Model

Give thanks in all circumstances, for this is God's will for you in Christ Jesus. Do not put out the Spirit's fire; do not treat prophecies with contempt. Test everything. Hold on to the good.

1 Thessalonians 5:18-21

The Bible tells us to *"test everything."* The purpose of the next two chapters is to test or examine the current traditional understanding of the biblical plan of salvation. This understanding has been prevalent in Christian denominations for centuries and is usually expressed or explained using legal, criminal court system metaphors and language. Because of that we will refer to this traditional view or model as the "legal model."

The science and experience of salvation is something that can't easily be put into words. Like the taste of a certain food, the only way you can know for sure what it tastes like is to experience it for yourself. Therefore, to help us explain and understand salvation we need the help of things like parables, allegories, and metaphors.

The scriptures provide a number of these helps. But all allegories, parables, and metaphors have their limitations and if taken beyond those limitations error will be the result. This is the reason it would be beneficial for us to examine the traditional legal model of the plan of salvation carefully to determine if that is not the case with it. If we find that it is, and if we find there is a better model, the Church would certainly benefit from that knowledge.

When many Christians hear the word "legal," they immediately think of legalism; but I do not refer to the traditional model as "legal" because it is a "salvation by works" model, but rather because it is based on a legal, courtroom scenario with much of its legal operation and terminology.

I realize the things that we will examine here are considered sacred by many people and I do not take this lightly. But my questions are – Is this model true to the Scriptures? Has it been pushed beyond its usefulness as a helpful model? And is there a better model that more clearly represents the true character of God and the plan of salvation?

For those living in the closing hours of earth's history, I believe these are important questions and only an honest, open-minded investigation of this model will help us find the answers. If the traditional legal model taught in the Church today is indeed the best model, then it will bear up under close scrutiny and those who place their faith in it have nothing to fear. But if it can't, we certainly need to be aware of that.

Is the legal model biblical? The Bible does contain legal terminology and imagery, especially of the book of Romans. But the fact is that much of the legal language in the Bible is be due more to translation than inspiration. A close look at the definitions of the original Hebrew and Greek words used in the Scriptures will reveal this fact. Another point is that the writers of the Bible had no knowledge of the kind of legal court system we are so familiar with here in the Western World of today.

What probably played the largest role in the heavy use of legal metaphors and language in religion took place during the period of history called the "Dark Ages." This period was called the Dark Ages because it was during this time that common people had little, if any, access to the Bible. To add to that, nearly all Bibles were required to be written in Latin, the language of Roman law which the common people in those times could not read or understand. As a result, without the light of God's Word, many philosophical (human) teachings that had no biblical basis became entrenched in the Church and embedded throughout its teachings. The result was the emergence of a corrupt religious system, that united with the power of the state, began to persecute and execute millions.

This increasing corruption and violence in Church leadership led many to call for reform. Leading out in the reformation movement were gifted leaders like William Tyndale, John Wycliffe, John Huss, Martin Luther, John Calvin and others; men whom it appears God was especially guiding back to the truths of His Word.

Soon the cry "sola scriptura," (the Latin slogan for "the Bible and the Bible only") was the cry of the Reformation. To great numbers of people the teachings of these men, especially Luther and Calvin, were seen as authoritative and eventually church denominations were established around their teachings.

These two men, Luther and Calvin, studied law but later decided to go into the ministry even though trained as lawyers, not as theologians. In spite of the belief of relying on the Bible only, orthodox Protestant Christianity has chosen to base many of its doctrines (beliefs/teachings) primarily on the understandings, writings and teachings of these men. During this period Calvin wrote a monumental four-volume work entitled, The Institutes of the Christian Religion which reached its final form in A.D. 1559. Calvin's teachings contained in these books have had an enormous impact on many major church bodies to this day. The doctrine of the immortality of the soul, the eternal suffering of the lost in hellfire and predestination are a few that can be traced back to Calvin's influence on the Church through his writings rather than coming from the Bible itself.

The King James Version of the Bible was translated during this period, (A.D. 1611), and likely its translators were strongly influenced by the writings of Calvin and Luther. Evidence of that can be seen in the use of many Latin legal words in that translation such as "justification," "sanctification," and "propitiation." These words were not the words of the Apostles which were originally written in Greek, not in Latin. Latin is the language heavily used to this day in the legal profession and was preferred by John Calvin. So it should come as no surprise that we find a lot of legal terminology prevalent in this most popular and widely accepted version of the Bible and consequently incorporated into church doctrine. I believe that all of these factors played a major role in the development of the traditional legal model of the plan of salvation believed and taught by so many in the churches today.

In the next chapter we will examine the major points of the traditional legal model.

Chapter Five

A Closer Look at the Legal Model

Do your best to present yourself to God as one approved, a workman who does not need to be ashamed and who correctly handles the word of truth.

2 Timothy 2:15

In this chapter we will begin taking some key points of the legal model of the plan of salvation and examining them closely using the Bible and logic as our guide. As we do, we want to either confirm or determine if there is sufficient reason to question each point.

In the legal model God is viewed as the Sovereign Supreme Ruler and Creator of all things in heaven and earth. Using the Bible as our source of truth, there is no reason to doubt or question this. God *is* Creator and the Supreme Sovereign Power in the universe. Isaiah says –

"Before me no god was formed, nor will there be one after me. I, even I, am the LORD, and apart from me there is no savior."[1]

In Colossians Paul declares – *"For by him all things were created: things in heaven and on earth, visible and invisible, whether thrones or powers or rulers or*

---

1   - Isaiah 43:10-11

authorities; all things were created by him and for him. He is before all things, and in him all things hold together. "[2]

In this model God, being Creator and Ruler of the universe, has the right to establish and command that His Law be obeyed by all. The Ten Commandment Law given on Mt. Sinai by God Himself embodies principles that describe the moral behavior God desires of men and women. One problem here however is that some religious institutions have taken it upon themselves to change this Law by taking out some commandments and modifying others. Others have claimed that keeping this Law is legalistic, that the Commandments no longer apply to the believer because they have been "nailed to the cross" thereby abolishing them altogether. All this seems questionable as well as illogical when you realize that implies that commands like *"Thou shall not kill"* or *"Thou shall not steal"* could somehow be modified or abolished! Therefore some discussion is in order here because of the confusion about how Christians are to relate to God's Law.

The key question is – why did God give the Law in the first place? Is He arbitrary – that is, does God demand that we behave in the way He has chosen for us for no other reason than just because He said so?

---

2 - Colossians 1:16-17

In Galatians we find that very question, *"What, then, was the purpose of the law?"* Then it answers, *"it was added because of transgressions."*[3] In other words, God gave the Law because people were behaving in disorderly and harmful ways, hurting themselves and others. Paul confirms this in his letter to Timothy –

"We also know that law is made not for the righteous but for lawbreakers and rebels, the ungodly and sinful, the unholy and irreligious; for those who kill their fathers or mothers, for murderers...."[4]

A modern day example would be traffic laws. If everyone today drove their cars in a safe manner, always yielding the right of way to other drivers, never driving carelessly or too fast, always stopping at stop signs, never doing anything that would put themselves or others in danger on the roads, would there be any need for the state to legislate laws regulating drivers? No, but we all know it's not that way. Many people drive in a way that is dangerous to themselves and others, so we must have laws to regulate behavior behind the wheel for the good of all.

Now in the same way, if the people God called out of Egypt back in Moses' day were loving God with all their

---

3   - Galatians 3:19
4   - 1 Timothy 1:9

heart and their neighbor as themselves there would have been no need for God to "lay down the law" at Mt. Sinai. But the Bible says the people Moses brought out of Egypt were *"stiff-necked."* This term is translated from a Hebrew word meaning they were hard, cruel, severe, obstinate, and difficult. We can liken God's situation to that of parents who have strong willed, misbehaving children with whom they must "lay down the law" in order to bring about peace and harmony in the family, not to be arbitrary or "show the kids who's boss," but for the good of the children.

If God is as we believe and how the Bible presents Him to be, the very essence of love and compassion, righteous, all-wise, seeing the end from the beginning, all knowing – if God is all this and He says we should do this or do that and not do the other, it is not legalism to do what He says, it just makes good sense! Deuteronomy tells us: *"The LORD commanded us to obey all these decrees and to fear the LORD our God, so that we might always prosper and be kept alive, as is the case today."*[5] God gave His Law for our good always! If that is true, why would anyone want to change or do away with it as some have attempted to do?

---

5   - Deuteronomy 6:24

Since the Bible clearly says the Law was given for our good always, then any violation of that Law, regardless of who the violator might be, will bring about suffering and pain. Therefore we can define sin as rebellion against or disregard for, God's good Law of love – love for Him and love for one another. Therefore, this point is valid if understood correctly.

Next, from the legal model perspective, God being the Law giver has also determined penalties for violations of His Law. These penalties include various kinds of suffering, pain, and death, with the ultimate and final penalty being the "second death."[6] Often I have heard the expression "God's gonna get you for that!" Many days in my own life, there seemed to be a dark cloud hanging over my mind when I knew I had done wrong and I wondered what God was going to do to punish me. And many times when things went badly I thought, "I wonder what sin I have committed that God is punishing me this way?"

In the book The Desire of Ages we find an interesting comment –

"It is true that all suffering results from the transgression of God's law, but this truth had become perverted. Satan, the author of sin and all its results, had led men to look upon

---

6   - Revelation 20:6, 14

disease and death as proceeding from God,--as punishment arbitrarily inflicted on account of sin."[7]

It is true that God, being the Creator of all things, has established laws or principles that operate in both the physical and spiritual realms. But these laws are all in harmony with His nature which is unconditional, unselfish love. Having established these laws, there are consequences for their violation; otherwise they would cease to be laws. Is the penalty for sin an arbitrary, externally inflicted punishment like we see administered in our court systems? Or is the punishment for sin, rather than an arbitrary, imposed penalty, simply the natural consequences of our own choices and actions? Our answer to this question will greatly affect our concept of God's character which will in turn ultimately shape our own character and destiny.

As stated previously, God has established certain principles of law in both the physical and spiritual realms. But if a law is not arbitrary the penalty wouldn't be either. Therefore we must conclude the "penalty" is determined by the principle of cause and effect, sowing and reaping. Every action has a sure and certain consequence. Right actions will result in good consequences – wrong actions will result in bad consequences.

---

7 - Desire of Ages p. 471

Take the law of gravity for example. The law of gravity is God's law. He put it in place for our good. Without it we would all float away. If a person, either ignoring or in defiance of the law of gravity jumps out of an airplane at 12,000 feet without a parachute, gravity will pull them rapidly to the ground and the impact will likely kill them. God does not punish this person for breaking His law of gravity. Rather, the "punishment" comes as the natural consequence of jumping out of the airplane and gravity pulling them rapidly to the earth. Do you see the point? God did not punish them; rather the violation of law inherently resulted in the painful and deadly "penalty" as an unavoidable, natural consequence.

Just as in the natural realm, so it is in the spiritual realm. There are certain consequences from violation of God's spiritual laws. These violations are called "sin." The biblical word for sin is defined as "missing the goal or missing the path of right." Sin is refusing to do what one knows is good and right. The Bible tells us that *"Anyone, then, who knows the good he ought to do and doesn't do it, sins."*[8]

The real problem is, when God's Laws are violated someone always gets hurt. Sin hurts the one who violates

8 - James 4:17

the Law as well as the one who is subjected to the violation. And what we often overlook is that in every case God, who loves us so deeply, is also hurt by our sin.

We may seem to get by for a while but the Bible says, *"you may be sure that your sin will find you out."*[9] Sooner or later the natural consequence of breaking God's good Law will come. Paul clearly states – *"Do not be deceived: God cannot be mocked. A man reaps what he sows."*[10]

I believe that long ago God looked into the future and saw that certain types of behavior would result in cruelty, hatred, pain, disease, and death. God said, these things are evil; don't do these things; I don't want to see you hurt. Then God looked again and saw that certain other types of behavior would bring forth peace, harmony, love and life and God said, these things are right; do these things and live.

I realize this line of thinking may be new to some, but please hear me out. The Bible does say that God *"does not leave the guilty unpunished."*[11] But that does not mean that God will personally impose punishments on the guilty. It is in God's design that the natural consequences of sin

---

9   - Numbers 32:23
10 - Galatians 6:7
11 - Exodus 34:7

punish the guilty; sin punishes sinners. Even King David, a man after God's own heart suffered the consequences of his sin even though he was forgiven by God. We cannot escape the consequences of our actions and attitudes. God established the law or principle of sowing and reaping and God does not change this law. But if given permission, God can transform sinners so that they come to stop their sin; and when the sin is stopped there will no longer be painful consequences.

The fact is that there are passages in the Bible that do indicate that God does not personally punish the sinner. For example David says –

"He does not treat (punish) *us as our sins deserve or repay us according to our iniquities."*[12] And Paul reminds us *"that God was reconciling the world to himself in Christ, not counting men's sins against them."*[13]

These are just a couple of the verses that provide evidence that God does not impose external punishment on the violators of His law, because as we have already discussed, punishment is the natural consequence or result of sinful actions. Sin punishes sin!

---

12 - Psalm 103:10
13 - 2 Corinthians 5:19

The Bible says *"Then, after desire has conceived, it gives birth to sin; and sin, when it is full-grown, gives birth to death."*[14] Notice, it is sin that brings death, not God. It is the natural outworking of the consequences of the continued violation of the law of good.

However clear this may be, in the legal model this concept is rejected or largely ignored. In the legal model God is viewed as imposing a legal, external and arbitrary punishment against sin as the Divine Judge and Executioner. The legal model actually makes God out to be more feared than sin itself! I believe we have reason to question the use of the legal model on this point.

Finally, the Bible says there will be a future day of judgment when the final consequences of sin and how God has related to it will be clearly seen by all. And most importantly, that will be a day in which God's name – His reputation and character – will be vindicated and when everyone experiences the final consequences and rewards from their choices in this life.

I don't know how many times when this issue is discussed that I have heard someone declare, "Yes, God is a loving God, but He is also 'just.'" By this they infer that God must see to it that those guilty of breaking His Law

---

14 - James 1:15

must pay the full penalty owed. Then, in order for humans guilty of violating His law to be released from that penalty God must forgive them. Being "just" He cannot simply forgive sinners without the penalty being paid in some way, so He sent His Son to take the sinner's place to suffer their penalty by dying on the cross. This is seen as somehow legally enabling God to forgive the sinner and still remain "just." However under this model, even though Jesus has paid the penalty in full, pardon is still only granted on the basis of a person's acceptance of Jesus' sacrifice for them.

There are things we need to take a closer look at on this point as well. The key objective and focus of the legal model is *being forgiven*. Though the statement cannot be found in the Bible, we often read or hear someone say, *"Jesus died so God could forgive us for our sins."* In a Bible study guide published by a large church denomination entitled "The Perfect Escape," two statements are made in bold print – **"Sin can be forgiven only by death"** and **"When Jesus died, all our sins were forgiven."**

I realize these may be comforting words for many Christians, but let's look at this carefully and honestly for what these statements are really implying. This is assuming that God requires death before He will forgive, and the death of Jesus somehow met that requirement! That means it must be terribly hard for God to forgive us! Apparently many theologians agree with this. For example, a professor at a theological seminary in Michigan wrote in an article entitled, "The Dynamics of Forgiveness" the following statement: *"Forgiveness is tough even for God. The sanctuary service teaches us that God cannot forgive without sacrifice."*[15]

God cannot forgive without sacrifice? I do not question the faith of those who say these kinds of things, but I can't help but wonder if statements such as this have been thoroughly and carefully thought through. I wonder if they have considered how God's character is negatively impacted by these comments. Please follow me carefully on this point. What obviously has not been considered is that statements such as these, though I am certain was unintended by those who made them, imply that Satan is correct; that God (the Father) is not merciful and that it is hard for Him to forgive, so hard that in order for Him to forgive that He must be appeased with a blood sacrifice. But the sacrifice of animals was not sufficient; they only pointed to what He ultimately required, a human sacrifice.

---

15 - www.biblicalperspectives.com/endtimeissues/eti_92.html

But not just any human sacrifice would do; only a perfect, sinless human would suffice for such payment!

No matter how one may sugarcoat this idea, it implies that God must be similar to the ancient pagan gods who likewise demanded blood sacrifices before they would forgive or bless. The Bible says that God condemned the practices of the ancient pagans who sacrificed their children to pagan gods, yet much of Christianity today teaches that God sacrificed His own Son as a "propitiation" to appease Himself or to "atone" for our sin! It is taught that the death of Christ was necessary to satisfy God's "justice." Torturing and killing a perfectly innocent man is somehow considered justice? Such twisted logic makes no sense! It's no wonder many people are confused about why Jesus had to die. Now note what the Bible does say –

"For I (God) desire mercy, not sacrifice, and acknowledgment of God rather than burnt offerings."[16] And in Psalms David states, *" Sacrifice and offering You did not desire; My ears You have opened. Burnt offering and sin offering You did not require"*[17] (NKJV). And in Matthew Jesus says – *"But if you had known what this means, 'I*

---

16 - Hosea 6:6
17 - Psalm 40:6 NKJV

desire mercy and <u>not sacrifice</u>,' you would not have condemned the guiltless."[18]

These verses clearly say that God does not desire or require sacrifice! Why then were they called for in the Temple ceremonies? Why does the Bible say, *"without shedding of blood there is no remission"*[19]? Allow me to answer that question with another question: Was the shedding of the blood of a sacrifice, whether it be the blood of an animal or the blood of Jesus, necessary to change God? Did the sacrifice cause God to love and forgive when He would not have done so otherwise? ***Or***, was the shedding of blood necessary in order to change us sinners? Was the sacrifice made to soften the sinner's hardened heart by demonstrating God's love and thus winning us back to trust or faith in God?

As bad as it speaks of us humans, it became necessary for Jesus to die because there was no other way for God to get through to us – to get us to realize He loves us unconditionally! The Bible repeatedly states that God does not change! The blood was shed to change us, to appease us – sinful rebels, not to appease God! It was to reconcile us back to God, not God back to us! How

---

18 - Matthew 12:7
19 - Hebrews 9:22 NKJV

wonderful of God that He was willing to do something this drastic to reach us! One of my favorite authors, E. G. White, states this quite clearly:

"The atonement of Christ was not made in order to induce God to love those whom He otherwise hated; and it was not made to produce a love that was not in existence; but it was made as a manifestation of the love that was already in God's heart...we are not to entertain the idea that God loves us because Christ has died for us, but that He so loved us that He gave His only-begotten Son to die for us."[20]

Another phrase often quoted by the adherents to the legal model is, *"Jesus died to pay for all my sins."* Just as in the previous statement, *"Jesus died so God could forgive us,"* this statement cannot be found anywhere in the Bible. And think about this: If Jesus died to pay a "legal" penalty for our sin, and the legal penalty is to burn in hell for eternity, the penalty has not really been paid! Jesus is not burning in hell for eternity!

Even if the legal penalty is to suffer in flames, being burned alive for as long as we deserve and then finally die

---

20 - Signs of the Times, May 30, 1895

as others teach, the penalty has still not been paid! Jesus was not burned alive!

If the legal penalty is the Second Death or eternal separation from God, the penalty was not paid either because He was resurrected and is now with the Father!

As we begin to think this through more clearly, this point in the legal model raises serious issues. Again follow me carefully. If by Christ's death my sins are paid for in full, whether I accept it or not does not change the fact that the penalty or price has been paid. If Christ's death was a *"once for all"* legal payment for sin, it would only seem logical that all people would then be saved whether they accepted it or not! Their debt or penalty having been paid, no further payment or action should be required since the debt no longer exists! Though it may be a wonderful thought, this idea is not realistic and would never hold up in any court of law.

Adherents of the legal model seem to have failed to recognize the difference between civil and criminal law. Civil law permits substitute payment. Your auto insurance company may pay to repair the damage done by your wrongful act. But criminal law demands that the one who committed the crime pay the penalty for it. Imagine a person guilty of mass murder and as he stands before the judge he is sentenced to death. Another person in the court room arises and says, "Your Honor, I will die in his place, set him free."

Are we really to believe that the judge would allow that? We all know full well that no judge in the world would allow that! This type of story has been told many times to illustrate God's pardon of sinners, but this is carrying the legal model to the point of absurdity, far beyond what it was intended to convey.

Another problem with this idea is that it detracts from the fact that the suffering of Christ was never meant to be understood as a one time "legal" payment for sin. Rather Christ is to be seen as *"the Lamb that was slain from the creation of the world."*[21] This means that Christ has suffered the heart wrenching agony of the cross, not just one day 2000 years ago but every day since sin began; and it will not end until sin is no more. Since the first sin in the Garden of Eden, every time a person willfully sins they crucify the Son of God all over again![22] Consider the following statement:

"Few give thought to the suffering that sin has caused our Creator. All heaven suffered in Christ's agony; but that

---

21 - Revelation 13:8
22 - see Hebrews 6:6

suffering did not begin or end with His humanity. The cross is a revelation to our dull senses of the pain that, from its very beginning, sin has brought to the heart of God. Every departure from the right, every deed of cruelty, every failure of humanity to reach his ideal, brings grief to Him. "[23]

Read these words again – *"The cross is a revelation to our dull senses of the pain that, from its very beginning, sin has brought to the heart of God."* I believe this is what the Bible means when it says Christ was *"the Lamb that was slain from the creation of the world."* God has suffered since the very first sin! Reminds me of a song that goes something like this: *"Each time I fail, I swing the hammer that drives the nail."* God continues to suffer as we continue to willfully sin.

The truth is, Jesus did not die to pay for our sin, to take our place because someone **had** to die, either Him or us. Nor did He die so that God would forgive us. These legal propositions cheapen the most magnificent demonstration of love the world will ever see. The cross was the *only way* that God could draw everyone to Himself. The cross was the *only way* that God could demonstrate His

---

23 - Education p. 263

love in such fashion that men and even angels would come to fully trust Him again. The cross was the *only way* to expose Satan's lies about God. As one biblical commentator wrote:

"Without shedding of blood there is no remission for sin. He must suffer the agony of a public death on the cross, that witness of it might be borne without the shadow of a doubt."[24]

"That witness of it might be borne," in other words, human beings have to see something that dramatic, that shocking to enable them to see their own sinful, selfish condition in contrast with God's infinite and unselfish love for them. This is exactly what Jesus was referring to in John 12 *"When I am lifted up from the earth, I will draw everyone to me.' (In saying this he indicated the kind of death he was going to suffer)."*[25]

And this is why Peter wrote, *"For Christ died for sins once for all, the righteous for the unrighteous, to bring you to God. He was put to death in the body but made alive by the Spirit."*[26]

---

24 - E. G. White, Manuscript 101, 1897
25 - John 12:32 GNB
26 - 1 Peter 3:18

Christ sacrificed Himself, not to pay a legal penalty to appease or change God's attitude towards us but to change us, to win us back to trust in God so that God can change us, heal us, save us.

The sinless angels needed the cross too – but not for forgiveness. They had never sinned; they didn't need to be "covered by the blood." Paul says in Colossians –

"For God was pleased to have all his fullness dwell in him, and through him to reconcile to himself all things, whether things on earth or things in heaven, by making peace through his blood, shed on the cross."[27]

Note this thoughtful comment – *"It is through the efficacy* (effectiveness) *of the cross that the angels of heaven are guarded from apostasy. Without the cross they would be no more secure against evil than were the angels before the fall of Satan. Angelic perfection failed in heaven. Human perfection failed in Eden, the paradise of bliss. All who wish for security in earth or heaven must look to the Lamb of God."*[28]

The only place men or angels will see the clear demonstration of the depth of God's love is at the Cross.

---

27 - Colossians 1:19-20
28 - Signs of the Times, September 30, 1889

Yet notwithstanding all we have discussed here, the key objective of the legal model remains forgiveness. In that model, the most important focus is always on, "What must I do so that God will forgive me?" But Jesus says – *"I tell you the truth, no one can see the kingdom of God unless he is born again."*[29]

Jesus did not say *"unless a man is forgiven"* but rather, *"no one can see the kingdom of God unless he is born again."* This is a big difference! As important as our need for forgiveness is in order to relieve us of our guilt, forgiveness alone cannot heal the damage caused by sin, nor can being forgiven save us or alleviate the consequences of our sins.

The key objective in salvation is conversion and regeneration resulting in a permanent change of heart and character. There must be a turning away from our selfish, sinful nature and a turning to God for deliverance from, and an overcoming of our sin; this is crucial.

I am reminded of a story I once heard about Isaiah and King Manasseh. This story is partly fictitious but it makes a good point. The story goes something like this:

---

29 - John 3:3

King Manasseh was one of the most wicked kings that reigned over Judah. King Manasseh killed more than five hundred prophets of God. One day he captured the prophet Isaiah, put him in a hollow log and sawed him in half, of course killing him. The moment Isaiah died he entered into the state of unconsciousness the Bible calls "sleep", unaware even now of what transpired after his death. Isaiah doesn't know that sometime later King Manasseh was touched by the Holy Spirit and converted. On resurrection day they both are awakened at the Lord's coming and taken to heaven. One day Isaiah is walking down the streets of gold, turns a corner and lo and behold, he sees none other than King Manasseh! Isaiah, remembering what the king did to him goes running to the Lord and says, "Lord, do you know who I just saw? I just saw King Manasseh! Lord, you remember what he did! What is he doing here? And the Lord says to Isaiah, "Oh, its O.K. Isaiah, I pardoned him." Would that answer be very comforting to Isaiah? Is that what Isaiah needs to hear? No, Isaiah wants to know that Manasseh has a new heart and a right spirit, that he is a changed man who would never think of doing those things again![30]

---

30 - Story as told by A. Graham Maxwell

Do you see the problem with all the emphasis on forgiveness in the legal model? Simply being forgiven or pardoned does not repair the internal damage caused by sin. Forgiveness alone does little to change the heart or the character, and that deeper heart change is absolutely necessary for true salvation to be accomplished.

According to the legal model forgiveness is only granted on the basis of one's acceptance of Jesus' sacrifice in our place. There are those who declare that all that is necessary is for the sinner to *"only believe,"* for *"Jesus has done it all."* But the truth is that if I believe the gospel, and if I believe Jesus died for me while that belief does not motivate me to surrender my heart to God and cooperate with Him in bringing about a transformation for the better in my heart and life, then my believing is useless; it will only lead to presumption, hypocrisy and self-deception.

Presumption is another real danger in the legal model because of so much emphasis on forgiveness. Many, because they are forgiven believe they are saved no matter how they live from that point on. The "once saved, always saved" doctrine may have grown out of this idea. But even though a person is truly forgiven, if there is no real change in their heart and life they are still trapped in their sinful habits of thinking and they are still in reality unsaved, unfit and unsafe for the society of heaven.

The Bible says we are to *"grow in the grace and knowledge of our Lord and Savior Jesus Christ."*[31] But we won't grow if we do not keep learning more about our infinite, unchangeable, and gracious God. We can't put God in a box and say, "that is all there is." No, God is limitless and there is so much more for us to learn about Him and His ways. Isaiah says –

"'For my thoughts are not your thoughts, neither are your ways my ways,' declares the LORD. 'As the heavens are higher than the earth, so are my ways higher than your ways and my thoughts than your thoughts.'"[32]

We must begin to "think outside the box" of human assumptions. We must be careful we do not try to create God in our image but that we are restored into His.

The final point I will address is that in the legal model, whether one is ushered into the gates of paradise or cast into the lake of fire, the consequences are eternal in nature. On this point the Bible is clear; the consequences of the choices we make in life are eternal Therefore we must take sin and salvation very seriously now. However, there

---

31 - 2 Peter 3:18
32 - Isaiah 55:8

are many different ideas taught regarding what the Bible means when it speaks of eternal life or eternal death. In the legal model these are seen as rewards and punishments. But there is much more to it than that. (This will be discussed in detail in another chapter.) But even if there were no heaven or hell and this life is all there is, God's way of unselfish love is still the best way to live in this world.

As we close this chapter, after seeing so many problems with this legal model the question needs to be asked: Can this model be useful? What purpose could it serve? I believe we must consider the fact that many people have been ingrained with a picture of God as being the Judge and Executioner and that if they sin and reject Christ, God will severely punish them. Those who hold this view need this legal model to give them assurance that they can be forgiven in order to escape His wrath. They are comforted by believing that Jesus as their "advocate" or "lawyer," is interceding between them and God, that He is pleading His blood to appease the Father's anger. It may be that God can use this way of reaching these people where they are until they become open to a better understanding of Him and His way of saving people.

Understanding that, the legal model may have its place as a metaphor in God's overall plan. But as we more closely examine it point by point there is reason for serious concern. Viewing salvation in this way, the Trinity is seen as divided against itself with the Son pleading with a reluctant Father and sacrificing Himself in order to convince God to accept and forgive us. In this model there is more emphasis on forgiveness than regeneration, and views of God's character are distorted, which may be the most serious problem. I believe we must conclude it may not be the ideal model for Christians today.

From our investigation it is also clear that this model has been carried far beyond its limits as a useful metaphor. So, is there a better model that more clearly represents the true character of God and the plan of salvation that can be solidly supported in Scripture? The answer is yes there is, and we will introduce that model in the next chapter.

Chapter Six

Introducing the Healing Model

For this people's heart has become calloused; they hardly hear with their ears, and they have closed their eyes. Otherwise they might see with their eyes, hear with their ears, understand with their hearts and turn, and I would heal them.

Matthew 13:15

In the previous chapter we examined some of the key points of the traditional legal model of the plan of salvation. As we did, we found that most raised serious questions. We closed that chapter with the suggestion that there is a better model of the plan of salvation that is supported in Scripture. This model we will refer to as the "healing model."

In the healing model, sin is not seen as simply breaking the law for which punishment will be imposed similar to our judicial court system. In this model the sinner is not viewed as a condemned criminal; rather, in the healing model sin is seen as disorderly behavior resulting from a diseased heart and mind; an inherited illness that if not cured will cause the suffering and eventual death of its victim as a natural consequence of the disease itself.

In this model God is not viewed as the Judge and Executioner but rather as the Great Physician who alone is able to cure this deadly sickness and restore its victims to perfect health and ultimately life unending.

Before we begin examining this model I believe it is important that we confirm that it has a scriptural foundation. The following are some texts in which illustrate the plan of salvation in a healing model:

"I said, 'O LORD, have mercy on me; heal me, for I have sinned against you.'"[1]

"Heal me, O LORD, and I will be healed; save me and I will be saved."[2]

These two verses are written in a style known as Hebrew poetry. Instead of ending each sentence with words that rhyme as we do in English, in Hebrew poetry the second part of the sentence explains, clarifies, or restates what is said in the first part. The writers of both the previous verses are stating that being saved is like being healed. Now note the next one -

"But he was pierced for our transgressions, he was crushed for our iniquities; the punishment that brought us peace was upon him, and by his wounds we are healed."[3]

---

1   - Psalm 41:4
2   - Jeremiah 17:14
3   - Isaiah 53:5

"By his wounds we are healed." Common sense tells us that His suffering does not cure physical disease, but it can draw us toward Him and in so doing it can lead to recovery from, or healing of our sin-sick soul.

Most Christians are familiar with the New Testament term for salvation, the English word *"saved,"* translated from the Greek word *"sozo"* which means *"to be well,"* – *"to be whole"* or *"to be safe, to be saved or healed."* The translators of the King James Bible translated it with all three meanings. Note the following examples:

"My little daughter lieth at the point of death: I pray thee, come and lay thy hands on her, that she may be <u>healed</u> (sozo)."[4]

"For she said, If I may touch but his clothes, I shall <u>be whole</u> (sozo)."[5]

"It is easier for a camel to go through the eye of a needle, than for a rich man to enter into the kingdom of God. And they were astonished out of measure, saying among themselves, Who then can be <u>saved</u>? (sozo)."[6]

---

4 - Mark 5:23
5 - Mark 5:28
6 - Mark 10:25-26

These words – saved, healed, made whole – are all translated from same Greek word, "sozo." So when referring to salvation we could correctly say, *"I am healed"* or *"I am made whole"* instead of *"I am saved."*

As seen in the following examples in the New Testament, we see that Jesus also used the healing metaphor many times to illustrate salvation.

"It is not the healthy who need a doctor, but the <u>sick</u>. I have not come to call the righteous, but sinners."[7]

In this verse, Jesus likens the sinner to the sick who need a physician, who need healing.

"For this people's heart has become calloused; they hardly hear with their ears, and they have closed their eyes. Otherwise they might see with their eyes, hear with their ears, understand with their hearts and turn, and I would <u>heal</u> them."[8]

"I would heal them." The Greek word translated *"heal"* in this verse has only one meaning and that is, "to cure." This obviously is not physical healing Jesus is referring to in this verse but rather spiritual healing of the sin-sick soul.

---

7   - Mark 2:17

8   - Matthew 13:15

I believe these Bible verses are clear evidence that the healing model is used throughout Scripture. It has been my experience that once a person is introduced to the healing model, a whole new world of understanding begins to open up for them. The Grace of God and His marvelous plan of salvation to restore man back into the image of God in which he was first created are brought clearly into view. Not only that, but we are introduced to a new and enlightening picture of God, a God in whom there is nothing to fear – ever! We begin to see and understand more fully His perfect love that *"drives out fear."*[9] And, just as a physician would not punish or destroy his patients, we see a God who does not arbitrarily punish or destroy, but a God whose greatest desire is in healing and saving sinners. In this model we learn that the thing we must fear most is not God, but rather clinging to our sinful feelings of pride and self-sufficiency, refusing to come and cooperate with the Great Physician so that He may heal us.

Now, in the next chapter, we will, as we did with the legal model, examine each point.

---

9 - 1 John 4:18

Chapter Seven

Examining the Healing Model

But for you who obey me, my saving power will rise on you like the sun and bring healing like the sun's rays. You will be as free and happy as calves let out of a stall.

Malachi 4:2 GNB

In this chapter we will examine the key points of the healing model and also provide further evidence to support and better understand this model.

In the healing model just as in the legal model, God is seen as the Almighty Creator who created all things in heaven and earth. He created mankind in His own image. God cared deeply for man and provided all that was needed for his peace and happiness. However, God has a cruel and powerful enemy, Satan, who deceived the first humans and infected them with a rebellious spirit of heart and mind.

In the book of Genesis we find the record of the creation of the earth and the tragic fall of our first parents, Adam and Eve. God created them as fully-grown, mature humans. He created every cell and organ in their bodies. God implanted within their hearts and minds His law of unselfish love. At the same time He created them with free will, the power to think and to do, to reason and learn and make choices. He created them with the ability to procreate, to have children of their own. God told them to be fruitful and multiply and fill the earth. In the beginning they were in complete harmony with God and the angels. Every day God came in person to the Garden and walked with them in the cool of the day.

One fateful day Eve found herself at the Tree of the Knowledge of Good and Evil which God had warned them not to eat from. There at the tree she heard the voice of a serpent speaking to her, *"Did God really say, 'You must not eat from any tree in the garden'?"* To which Eve replied – *"We may eat fruit from the trees in the garden, but God did say, 'You must not eat fruit from the tree that is in the middle of the garden, and you must not touch it, or you will die.'"* To which the serpent made this bold rebuttal, *"You will not surely die..., for God knows that when you eat of it your eyes will be opened, and you will be like God, knowing good and evil."*[1]

Eve had listened to God. She was clear on what He had warned them of; she repeated it almost word for word. But now as she listens to the serpent she begins to give serious consideration to what he is saying to her. Satan speaking through the serpent said that God had lied, that He couldn't be trusted, and to defy or to rebel against what God

---

1 - Genesis 3:1-5

had said was harmless and would not result in their death. He claimed that to the contrary it would enlighten and make them wise. Then, *"knowing good and evil,"* that is, knowing right from wrong for themselves, they would become like God and would no longer need Him to tell them what was right or wrong or what to do or not do.

I would venture to guess that Satan said to Eve something like this – "Death is something God is trying to frighten you with. There is no such thing as death! We are all immortal! Have you ever seen death? Have you ever heard of anyone dying? No, and no one else has either. God is just trying to frighten you so that you will remain a slave to His wishes."

In his twisted mind Satan may have convinced himself he was actually telling the truth, because up to that time there had been no death in the entire universe. Here is where I believe Eve found an excuse to doubt God's word. There was nothing God could point to and say, "This is what death is." There was no real evidence; just God's word. The more Eve thought about it, the more she became convinced that maybe the serpent was right after all. Finally her mind was made up; she saw no danger, only the possibility of exalting herself. She ate of the forbidden tree; we all know the rest of the story.

After Eve ate, she gave to Adam and he ate. They didn't notice anything at first, but later when God came to visit them in the cool of the day they found themselves afraid of Him. They had never been afraid before. They also suddenly realized they were "naked," that is they felt exposed and vulnerable; for the first time in their lives they felt guilt and shame. When God asked them about it they began to shift the blame for their actions. Adam blamed Eve (and God); Eve blamed the serpent. Now it became evident they had radically changed. They were experiencing feelings and demonstrating attitudes they had never had before.

When Adam and Eve made the decision to eat of the Tree of the Knowledge of Good and Evil, it was more than simply **doing** something God told them not to do. A radical change in perspective took place within their hearts and minds and they could never be the same.

The damage created in their minds was not imaginary; it was caused by the very real infection of deception that produces disorderly and destructive behaviors like lying, stealing, false witnessing, murder, and eventually results in the death of its victims. The very first human couple were infected in the Garden of Eden. Since then this disease has been passed from generation to generation. Now all human beings in this world are born infected with this rebellious, selfish spirit through no choice of their own. Note the following comment –

"Man was originally endowed with noble powers and a well-balanced mind. He was perfect in his being, and in harmony with God. His thoughts were pure, his aims holy. But through disobedience, his powers were perverted, <u>and selfishness took the place of love.</u> His nature became so weakened through transgression that it was impossible for him, in his own strength, to resist the power of evil. He was made captive by Satan, and would have remained so forever had not God specially interposed. It was the tempter's purpose to thwart the divine plan in man's creation, and fill the earth with woe and desolation."[2]

"*Selfishness took the place of love.*" What a tragedy! All one has to do is look at the history of man to see the horrible effect that this infection has had on the world since that time. Today each one of us has suffered in many ways because of great evils arising from selfishness. Selfishness is the root of all sin. Things like envy, jealously, hate, cheating, lying, stealing, adultery, murder, and all other harmful, hurtful behaviors are simply the outward

---

2   - God's Amazing Grace, p. 313

manifestation of the inner sickness of the self-centered mind. It is this self-centered tendency that causes us to rebel against God. If you think it through any sin you can name can be traced back to selfishness; my wants – my needs – my rights!

The Bible says in Romans, *"Therefore, just as sin entered the world through one man, and death through sin, and in this way death came to all men, because all sinned--"*[3] In other words, we are all born with a selfish, rebellious nature inherited from Adam and Eve. That nature, fallen, sinful human nature if allowed to take its natural course always results in ruin and death.

Because selfishness is harmful and destructive and had taken such deep root in the nature of our first parents, God sent Adam and Eve out of the Garden of Eden. No longer having access to the Tree of Life they were destined to eventually die. When God told them earlier they would die if they ate of the tree, it was not a threat as if He would have to execute them for disobedience to His command. Rather than a threat, it was a warning – a warning that if they chose to go against what He said they should do they were actually cutting themselves off from the only source of life and they would die as a consequence. The fruit of

---

3   - Romans 5:12

the Tree of the Knowledge of Good and Evil in a sense acted like a deadly poison in their souls.

There is a lesson in this for us all. If we disregard God's Word, feeling that we are self-sufficient and that we have the ability to determine for ourselves what is right and wrong, that we can go on our merry way without God; then we too are cutting ourselves off from the *"Tree of Life"* and we will eventually perish.

Let me stress once again; in the healing model death is seen as the natural consequence of rebellion against God in that we cut ourselves off from the only source of life; we unplug our own life support system so to speak. But in the legal model we are executed for disobedience at God's direction as He orders the sinner be cast into the lake of fire. But the Bible is very clear about this – it plainly states,

"But each one is tempted when, by his own evil desire (selfishness), *he is dragged away and enticed. Then, after desire* (selfishness) *has conceived, it gives birth to sin; and sin, when it is full-grown, gives birth to death."*[4]

Because the root of sin is in the mind, it is really more like insanity. The mind is the "control center" of our entire being. Within our minds are developed those things

---

4   - James 1:14,15

that make up our distinctive characters. Someone once said, "The mind is like a computer; GIGO, garbage in – garbage out." Because of the "garbage" that most humans feed into their minds the human race is on a perilous path. As we look back at the history of man, we can see that this is true. Many of the practices, attitudes, and lifestyles people enjoy are in reality destructive in the end. Yet knowing that, they continue to cling to those things, refusing to give them up, and that is insanity!

How about you? Is there something in your life that has proven to be hurtful to you or others, maybe even your family, yet you will not give it up? Remember, the Bible says – *"the whole head is sick."*[5] Aren't we all *"touched in the head"* to some extent, refusing to give up some cherished thing that is working our destruction? It is insane, yet many of us do it!

Many self-help books have been written on the countless ways that man has developed in attempts to rid himself of self-destructive behavior. After thousands of years it is painfully clear that humankind is not capable of healing themselves of this deeply rooted problem.

This is not only a problem for man but for our Creator as well. The Bible says in Isaiah –

5 - Isaiah 1:5

"So he became their Savior. In all their distress he too was distressed, and the angel of his presence saved them. In his love and mercy he redeemed them; he lifted them up and carried them all the days of old."[6]

God cares deeply for His children. Just as a parent suffers when his child is stricken with a horrible disease and can find no rest or peace as long as his child suffers; so our Heavenly Father suffers with us. In all our afflictions He is afflicted! God will have no rest or peace until this nightmare of sin that sickens, maims and destroys His children is over. When we go to God for forgiveness, what we should remember is this: sin is not about breaking God's law and making Him angry; rather it is breaking His heart and making Him hurt!

In the healing model, seeing sin as insanity helps us understand the words Christ uttered as He was being crucified, *"Father, forgive them, for they do not know what they are doing."*[7] I want to emphasize that Christ's prayer was for those who were doing horrific things to Him. His is the perfect demonstration of unselfish love, of hating the sin while loving the sinner.

---

6 - Isaiah 63:8-9
7 - Luke 23:34

It would be similar to a child suffering from a serious mental disorder and behaving irrationally, even hurtfully. But because of the love the parents have for the child and realizing the child doesn't know what he's doing, they do not get angry with or punish the child. Rather, they patiently work with him and do all they can to help him.

I believe God sees us this way. He knows we are sin-sick, suffering from a serious mental disorder. We don't really know what we're doing and so He does not punish us but rather longs to help us. Read again in Psalm 103 –

"He does not treat us as our sins deserve or repay us according to our iniquities. For as high as the heavens are above the earth, so great is his love for those who fear him; as far as the east is from the west, so far has he removed our transgressions from us. As a father has compassion on his children, so the LORD has compassion on those who fear him; for he knows how we are formed, he remembers that we are dust."[8]

This helps us to understand what it means to hate the sin but love the sinner. When we see another person behaving badly, instead of looking at them as a great sinner we should remember they are behaving that way because

---

8   - Psalm 103:10-14

they have a serious mental disorder. They are not criminals, they are sick. They don't really know what they are doing. And the worse a person is behaving the sicker they are; and the sicker they are the more they need our help, not our condemnation! We all have this sickness and some are in worse condition than others. This is why the Bible says we should comfort one another, help one another, encourage one another instead of judging and criticizing one another.

God being able to see the end from the beginning planned for this emergency. The One who created the heavens and the earth from nothing can create in man a new heart and a right spirit. He is the great Physician who can heal all our diseases and afflictions, physical or spiritual.

"Blessed be the God and Father of our Lord Jesus Christ, who has blessed us with every spiritual blessing in the heavenly places in Christ, just as He chose us in Him before the foundation of the world, that we should be holy and without blame before Him in love."[9]

From this text it is clear that God had planned before the creation of the world a way to rescue those who, through no fault of their own are born in this sin infested

---

9   - Ephesians 1:3-4 NKJV

world. After his great sin David prayed this prayer as recorded in Psalm 51 – *"Hide your face from my sins and blot out all my iniquity. Create in me a pure heart, O God, and renew a steadfast spirit within me."*[10] The Lord God being the Almighty Creator is certainly able to create in us a clean heart and to repair any damage done to our hearts and minds.

Once we realize that we are sin-sick and that we cannot heal ourselves, we must find a good physician, one who is qualified to administer the remedy that will bring the healing we need. The Bible says –

"Then know this, you and all the people of Israel: It is by the name of Jesus Christ of Nazareth, whom you crucified but whom God raised from the dead, that this man stands before you healed. He is 'the stone you builders rejected, which has become the capstone.' Salvation is found in no one else, for there is no other name under heaven given to men by which we must be saved."[11] (sozo – healed)

"Praise the LORD, O my soul, and forget not all his benefits – who forgives all your sins and heals all your

---

10 - Psalm 51:9-10
11 - Acts 4:10-12

diseases, who redeems your life from the pit and crowns you with love and compassion.[12]

Jesus Christ is the Great Physician who can heal all our diseases! But in order for God to heal those afflicted with this terrible disease there are certain things that must take place. The victim must be willing to come to Him trusting, that is, having faith in Him, believing that He knows what to do and is able to heal or save them. This is conversion, or the word some prefer is justification; the actual Greek word Paul used was "dikaioo" which means "to be set right." To be set right means a person has come to the place where they are no longer rebellious but are willing to listen and follow the Lord as best they can. When they are in that frame of mind the Lord can help and heal them.

To help illustrate this healing model I will use the example of an alcoholic. Medical science has learned that through no fault of their own some people are born with great potential for the disease of alcoholism in their DNA. For those in this condition it is almost impossible for them to control their drinking once they start; they are captive to their addiction. Yet many alcoholics are in denial and will

_____

12 - Psalm 103:2-4

not face the fact that they have a problem. In order for them to have any hope of recovery, they must first acknowledge or "confess" they have a problem. Once they admit they do have a problem they can begin to take corrective actions.

But even then, those who look within themselves for the power to quit soon realize they are helpless to overcome their addiction. It is at this point they must begin to seek help from other sources. Those who find the help they need and faithfully stick with the prescribed program, although they still have the alcoholic genes within their bodies and will as long as they live, these can overcome their addiction and live without alcohol. The alcoholic does not have to drink; they can overcome their addiction.

The sinner then, just as the alcoholic, is born with sin in his DNA. And just as with the alcoholic, it is impossible for him in his own strength to control his behavior. Man is held hostage to his selfish, sinful nature. Just as with the alcoholic, many people are in denial as to their sinful condition. But to have any hope of recovery they must first acknowledge or confess that they have a serious problem. This is why the Apostle John wrote, *"If we confess our sins, he is faithful and just and will forgive us our sins and purify us from all unrighteousness."*[13]

---

13 - 1 John 1:9

In the legal model many feel they must remember every sin they have ever committed and confess them one by one. That can be frightening because if they happen to forget one they feel they're in big trouble, for they are certain that every single sin must be named and repented of. Otherwise, any unconfessed sin will remain on heaven's books recorded as "unforgiven" and they are doomed. This is an enormous burden! But this is the effect of the legal model of thinking. This kind of religion makes God out to be demanding, harsh and seeking for excuses for us to be lost. But God is sympathetic and knows our weaknesses, He knows we can't possibly remember every little sin we have ever committed! But more seriously, this legal approach produces in us an antagonistic reaction to this kind of God when we feel we must compete against Him and purify ourselves in order for Him to accept us rather than simply trusting Him to do His work in us.

On the other hand, in the healing model what we need to confess is that we are sinners in need of help and healing, in need of forgiveness and cleansing from all our unrighteousness. The real meaning of the word *confession* is to come into agreement with someone. When we are willing to agree with the convictions of the Holy Spirit about our sins, we confess that His assessment of us is true instead of resisting or living in denial. But we can only do this after we begin to sense that God is not seeking to condemn us for our sins but desires to heal and save us from all our malfunctioning. The more we see Him as One who is waiting to heal us rather than to condemn us, the sooner we will be willing to trust Him enough to give Him full access to our hearts to begin that healing.

As previously stated, recognizing our condition and acknowledging it (agreeing with God) through confession is the first step in our recovery. Just as with the alcoholic, as long as we live in this corrupt body we will have the potential to sin. That's what John was referring to when he said, " *If we claim to be without sin, we deceive ourselves and the truth is not in us.* "[14]

In other words, no matter how much we have grown spiritually, if we say we don't have the potential to sin we are in denial. We are saying we are not sick, that we no longer have the infection of selfishness. But all of us, saved or lost, contain the bent to sin because we are all sinners by nature. We are living in corrupt fleshly bodies with inescapable selfish natures and we will be until Jesus comes. Only then will we become completely free of this fallen, selfish nature *"...In a moment, in the twinkling of an*

---

14 - 1 John 1:8

eye, at the last trumpet. For the trumpet will sound, and the dead will be raised incorruptible, and we shall be changed. For this corruptible must put on incorruption, and this mortal must put on immortality."[15]

The major difference between the saved and the lost is that the saved are participating in the recovery process and the lost are not; they remain in denial, or they are working hard attempting to heal themselves! Salvation is not an event, it is a process. As long as we are in the recovery process we can have the wonderful assurance of a completed salvation in the end. For the true meaning of the word *salvation* means to be salvaged, to have salve applied to a wound, to be restored, healed. As we cooperate with our Healer, our Salvaging expert, we can have full confidence that He can and will complete the work that He has started in us if we trust Him.

Again, using the example of the alcoholic, because we have the potential to sin, because we have selfishness in our DNA or genetic makeup does not mean that we have to sin any more than an alcoholic has to drink. According to the Bible we can be overcomers; but in order for us to overcome we need help – we cannot do it in our own strength. We need the Great Physician to heal the

---

15 - 1 Corinthians 15:52-53 NKJV

underlying issues that cause us to sin! According to the Word of God, He *"is able to keep you from falling and to present you before his glorious presence without fault and with great joy."[16]* I believe He can do what He says, how about you?

If we go to a physician with a serious medical problem, he may say we need to take some medication or do some sort of exercise or maybe even have surgery. If we refuse, we are likely not going to recover. In the same way, once we acknowledge our condition and come to the Great Physician for treatment we must have enough trust or faith in Him to be willing to do the things He prescribes. If we are unwilling to do those things He says are needed, we will not get well; we will not be saved or healed! This is what is called "saving faith"; trusting God enough to do those things He says we need to do.

You may remember the words of Christ to the rich young ruler, *"If you want to enter life, obey the commandments."[17]* I found it interesting that the word "commandment" is translated from the Greek word "entole" and it can be defined as an "authoritative prescription." In other words, something prescribed by one

---

16 - Jude 24
17 - Matthew 19:17

who is an expert authority such as a physician. That expert authority can be no one other than God when it comes to salvation (healing of the sin-sick soul).

By pointing this out, I am not advocating salvation by works here. Rather, in this model the works are those which come as a natural result or fruit of the relationship with, and faith in the Great Physician. Paul says it very clearly – *"For it is by grace you have been saved, through faith-- and this not from yourselves, it is the gift of God-- not by works, so that no one can boast. For we are God's workmanship, created in Christ Jesus to do good works, which God prepared in advance for us to do."*[18] Did you notice the words *"created in Christ Jesus to do good works"* Not, *"by"* good works, not *"with"* good works, but *"to do"* or *"for the purpose of"* good works!

The so-called faith in Christ that professes to release men from the obligation of obedience to God is not faith but presumption, a dead faith. *"By grace you have been saved, through faith."*[19] But *"faith by itself, if it is not accompanied by action, is dead."*[20]

Salvation is not about *what we do* as much as it is about *what we are*! We are all born defective. You might

---

18 - Ephesians 2:8-10
19 - Ephesians 2:8
20 - James 2:17

have heard the old saying, *"God loves you just as you are, but, He doesn't want to leave you that way."* While we do need forgiveness because of guilt, even more we need to _be transformed_ if we are going to be safe to live in heaven. (Remember the story of Isaiah and King Manasseh.) We cannot go into heaven clinging to our sin! We must be changed and change can be, and usually is, a difficult and sometimes painful process.

Theologians and preachers have come up with many theories about salvation to convince people that they can be saved without going through the painful process of change; that they can be saved without overcoming old, comfortable sinful habits. But that is a subtle and deadly deception. Remember the warning from Galatians –

"Do not be deceived: God cannot be mocked. A man reaps what he sows. The one who sows to please his sinful nature, from that nature will reap destruction; the one who sows to please the Spirit, from the Spirit will reap eternal life."[21]

And consider these promises from the book of Revelation –

"To him who overcomes, I will give the right to eat from the tree of life."[22]

---

21 - Galatians 6:7-8
22 - Revelation 2:7

"He who overcomes will not be hurt at all by the second death."[23]

"He who overcomes will, like them, be dressed in white. I will never blot out his name from the book of life."[24]

We cannot declare, "Jesus has done it all" and then sit back and expect to coast into heaven. We must, as the Apostle Paul admonished us, *"work out your salvation with fear and trembling."[25]* We must *"fight the good fight of the faith"[26]* if we are to enter into the gates of the beloved city of God. Again, this does not mean working our way into God's good graces. But we must take the time to spend with God so that He can do His transforming work in us. Finding time for this in our busy lives may be our greatest fight.

Jesus made very clear the steps we need to take as recorded in the gospel of Luke where Jesus said –

"Why do you call me, 'Lord, Lord,' and do not do what I say? I will show you what he is like who comes to me and hears my words and puts them into practice. He is like a man building a house, who dug down deep and laid the

23 - Revelation 2:11
24 - Revelation 3:5
25 - Philippians 2:12
26 - 1 Timothy 6:12

foundation on rock. When a flood came, the torrent struck that house but could not shake it, because it was well built. But the one who hears my words and does not put them into practice is like a man who built a house on the ground without a foundation. The moment the torrent struck that house, it collapsed and its destruction was complete."[27]

In this passage Jesus points out the three important steps to overcoming sin as we have outlined them in the healing model – 1) come to Me 2) Hear My words 3) and put them into practice.

Once a person has committed to cooperating with the Great Physician, they find that the process of healing begins to take effect immediately. Though they are not made completely well at once, as they continue to do their best by trusting and following His directions, they get better and better until at last when the Lord returns they find themselves in the very presence of God to live eternally. Jesus said very clearly in John 15 –

"Remain in me, and I will remain in you. No branch can bear fruit by itself; it must remain in the vine. Neither can you bear fruit unless you remain in me. I am the vine; you are the branches. If a man remains in me and I in him, he

---

27 - Luke 6:46

will bear much fruit; apart from me you can do nothing. If anyone does not remain in me, he is like a branch that is thrown away and withers; such branches are picked up, thrown into the fire and burned."[28]

Again, in the healing model if I am faithful to keep my appointments with the physician in charge of my case, if I am careful to follow his counsel, I will get well. In the same way, a believer should be careful to keep his appointments with the "Great Physician" with the most important appointment being the Sabbath. Then there are those daily appointments, the "quiet times" of devotion that are essential for keeping us spiritually "healthy" day by day.

The recovering believer is careful to follow the prescribed directions of the Great Physician, following closely all the counsel found in His Word. This is called sanctification, or to use a simpler term, "being kept right."

In the healing model, a person cooperates with the Great Physician so that the "cancer" of sin will go into remission. Then at the close of the investigative judgment, Christ will make an announcement – *"Let him who does wrong continue to do wrong; let him who is vile continue to be vile; let him who does right continue to do right; and let*

28 - John 15:4-6

him who is holy continue to be holy. Behold, I am coming soon! My reward is with me, and I will give to everyone according to what he has done."[29]

This is not a Judge declaring who is legally pardoned or who is condemned as in the legal model; rather, in the healing model this is the Great Physician's diagnosis of who has been healed and is safe to be granted entrance into the Kingdom of God.

On the other hand, those who have persistently refused to come to the Great Physician or who will not trust Him enough to follow His prescribed treatment will eventually die; but not only the death of sleep to which all the human race is subject, but ultimately the second death. However, God is not the one who stands as their executioner, but rather He *lets them go* to reap the consequences of their choices. They will then experience the awful second death, for the Bible says *"sin, when it is full-grown, gives birth to death."*[30] The Heavenly Father who has " *loved you with an <u>everlasting</u> love*"[31] will, just as a human parent, be terribly brokenhearted at the loss of His wayward children. He will weep over them as Jesus

---

29 - Revelation 22:11-12
30 - James 1:15
31 - Jeremiah 31:3

wept over Jerusalem long ago, but there is nothing more He can do. They have become incurable. But in the end the universe will finally be freed of the suffering, disease, pain, and death caused by sin while those who have been redeemed, saved and healed of the awful disease of sin will live eternally free.

Let me state once more: the healing model rather than being pre-occupied with forgiveness is focused on healing, restoration, the final overcoming of sin and becoming free of the consequences of it. God does not punish us for our sin-sick behavior. But He will at times allow the consequences of sin to bring us pain as a type of discipline so that we might come to our senses and turn away from our sin and turn to Him for help. He wants to help us stop the sin so that recovery can take place.

Do doctors kill their dying patients? Of course not! Rather, they do everything they can to save them. Then what about the Great Physician? What about God? Would He do any less? Does our Heavenly Father ever torture and kill His dying children? Of course not! It is sin itself that kills. As one author wrote, *"As leprosy was sure death if permitted to take its natural course, so the leprosy of sin will destroy the sinner* unless they received the healing of the grace of God.*"[32]*

God, our Gracious Father, rather than condemning us is desperately trying to save us. Not so He won't have to punish us but so that the cancer of sin will not destroy us! *"For the wages of sin is death, but the gift of God is eternal life in Christ Jesus our Lord.*"[33] Bottom line: Sin is the source of death and God is the source of life!

The following statement, in light of all the evidence available, adds more weight to the argument as to whether or not the wicked die at God's hand or as the natural consequence of sin.

"God does not stand toward the sinner as an executioner of the sentence against transgression; but he leaves the rejectors of his mercy to themselves, to reap that which they have sown. Every ray of light rejected, every warning despised or unheeded, every passion indulged, every transgression of the law of God, is a seed sown, which yields its unfailing harvest."[34]

---

32 - Signs of the Times, March 14, 1892
33 - Romans 6:23
34 - The Great Controversy, p. 37

"Leaving the rejectors of His mercy to themselves to reap that which they have sown" or to reap the consequences of their choices is a solid biblical principle.

"Do not be deceived: God cannot be mocked. A man reaps what he sows. The one who sows to please his sinful nature, from that nature will reap destruction; the one who sows to please the Spirit, from the Spirit will reap eternal life."[35]

When this view is presented the question always comes up, "But what about God's wrath?" The wrath of God is assumed by most people to be like man's wrath; but God says *"My ways are higher than your ways."*[36] Again, we must be careful we do not try to shape God in our image; He is not like us! In the next chapter we will study the wrath of God.

(The chart following on the next page, shows the contrast between the legal and healing models.)

---

35 - Galatians 6:7-8
36 - Isaiah 55:9

The Legal Model	The Healing Model
God is the Creator and as such has arbitrarily proclaimed His law by which mankind is to be governed and controlled.	God created the universe based on certain principles which are natural and immutable, love being the foundation.
An arbitrary, external pre-determined penalty will be visited upon those who disobey God's Law.	Violators of God's Law will suffer the natural consequence that result from violating the law/principle of unselfish love.
All humans are violators of the Law – all are born guilty and condemned to punishment and ultimately death.	All people are born infected with a rebellious, selfish nature which will eventually consume and destroy them if not remedied.
Those who do not repent and turn from their sinful behavior will be cast alive into a lake of fire. To avoid that, man must be pardoned / forgiven.	To avoid destruction, man must be healed of his deadly infection, forgiveness being only a part of that process.
Since man cannot save himself, the innocent Son of God came and paid the penalty for the guilty so God could justly pardon him.	Since man cannot heal himself, God sent His Son that by His life and death man may be won back to trust in God and thus be healed of their deadly infection.
A person who accepts Christ as Savior is pardoned and will not be punished but granted eternal life. Those who reject this offer are cast into the lake of fire.	If a person comes to God and co-operates with Him, he will be healed and can live eternally in God's life-giving presence.
God as Executioner will have all sinners cast into the lake of fire to be tormented forever, or at least as long as they deserve.	Those who refuse God's healing cut themselves off from the only source of life and will ultimately die the second death.

Chapter Eight

The Wrath of God

But my people would not listen to me; Israel would not submit to me. So I gave them over to their stubborn hearts to follow their own devices.

Psalms 81:11-12

We must let the Bible interpret itself to find the true understanding of the terms and phrases that it uses rather than depending on 'common usage' definitions – the assumptions and traditions that people have attached to them over the years. This was never more true than when it comes to grasping a correct understanding of God's wrath. Note the following biblical examples of how God's wrath works.

"On that day I will become angry with them and <u>forsake them; I will hide my face from them</u>, and they will be destroyed. Many disasters and difficulties will come upon them, and on that day they will ask, <u>'Have not these disasters come upon us because our God is not with us?'"</u>[1]

Why are evils and troubles befalling them? Because God is not among them – God has *given them up* to the

---

1   - Deuteronomy 31:17

consequences of their own choice to reject Him and follow their own ways. We see this again in another passage.

"But my people would not listen to me; Israel would not submit to me. So I gave them over to their stubborn hearts to follow their own devices."[2]

In the New Testament book of Romans Paul describes this same understanding of God's wrath. He gives those up who, disregarding His instruction and guidance for their good, persist in going their own way.

"The wrath of God is being revealed from heaven against all the godlessness and wickedness of men who suppress the truth by their wickedness, since what may be known about God is plain to them, because God has made it plain to them. For since the creation of the world God's invisible qualities-- his eternal power and divine nature-- have been clearly seen, being understood from what has been made, so that men are without excuse. For although they knew God, they neither glorified him as God nor gave thanks to him, but their thinking became futile and their foolish hearts were darkened. Although they claimed to be wise, they became fools and exchanged the glory of the immortal God for images made to look like mortal man and birds and

---

2   - Psalms 81:11-12

animals and reptiles. Therefore God gave them over in the sinful desires of their hearts.... They exchanged the truth of God for a lie, and worshiped and served created things rather than the Creator-- who is forever praised. Amen. Because of this, God gave them over to shameful lusts.... Furthermore, since they did not think it worthwhile to retain the knowledge of God, he gave them over to a depraved mind, to do what ought not to be done. "[3]

As previously stated, God's wrath is not like man's anger – getting mad and getting even. God's wrath rather, is God giving up or giving over – releasing those who insist on going their own destructive way, and as much as it breaks His heart, allows them to suffer the consequences of their own choices. God does not impose some external punishment upon them. He does not "beat them up" or "burn them up." Rather, after doing all He can to reach them, He will simply, yet sadly, give them over – release them to do what they want. As a result, in the end they reap the unpleasant results God has been trying to warn them against and prevent them from experiencing. When people persistently cut themselves off from the only Source of life and goodness – what will happen to them? They will inevitably suffer and eventually they will die.

---

3   - Romans 1:18-28

What one needs to do in order to understand how the wicked will die in the end is to go to the cross. Jesus died that death, experiencing the "wrath of God." If the wrath of God that punishes the sinner is "being given over," we should have texts that says Jesus was given over, and indeed we find them in Romans Chapter 4 and 8.

"He was <u>delivered over</u> to death for our sins and was raised to life for our justification."[4]

"What, then, shall we say in response to this? If God is for us, who can be against us? He who did not spare his own Son, but <u>gave him up</u> for us all-- how will he not also, along with him, graciously give us all things?"[5]

In both of these texts the word translated *"delivered over"* and *"gave Him up"* is the same Greek word we just read three times in Romans chapter one where it is translated *"gave them over."* The sense that He had been "given up" by God is what prompted the cry from Jesus' lips, *"My God, my God, why have you forsaken me?"*[6] Or in other words, *"Why have you given me up?"* Christ having been *"made sin for us"*[7] suffered the ultimate

---

4   - Romans 4:25
5   - Romans 8:31-32
6   - Matthew 27:46
7   - 2 Corinthians 5:21

consequences of sin on the cross. He experienced what the lost will experience at the Great White Throne Judgment, as they *"drink of the cup of the wrath of God."* That is, they experience the painful realization that they have cut themselves off from God, the only source of life, and instead of finding freedom and eternal life they see their portion is eternal death. They then experience an overwhelming, burning psychological pain from the despair, guilt, self-condemnation and anger they feel. As they become fully exposed, unshielded from the presence of God's purity and see clearly His passionate love for them, the resistance they have permanently ingrained in their hearts to that love will literally consume their life. Just as an electrical resistor overheats and bursts into flame when it encounters too much electrical power, similarly the wicked will experience overwhelming pain and at last death from the "heat" or tension produced by their own resistance to the love that pervades all of God's kingdom.

"Therefore I have poured out my indignation upon them; I have consumed them with the fire of my wrath; I have returned their conduct upon their heads, says the Lord GOD."[8]

---

8   - Ezekiel 22:31 NRSV

"I have returned their conduct upon their heads." In other words, God simply gives them over, releases them to experience the ultimate consequences of that which they have chosen. I believe the following sums up this idea.

"God destroys no man; but after a time the wicked are given up to the destruction they have wrought for themselves. When a man chooses his own way in the face of light and evidence, and refuses to be admonished, and to turn to the Lord with contrition of soul, the next message the Lord shall send will have less effect, for he allows his independent, self-willed spirit to control his judgment. He continues to cast the seed of resistance into his heart, and every time he repeats his act of resistance, refusing to turn from his own way to God's way, he bends his inclination in the way of disobedience, loves rebellion, and at last becomes callous, and the seed of unbelief ripens for the harvest."[9]

Yet when the subject of how God relates to the destruction of the wicked comes up, someone always asks – What about the flood? Doesn't that prove God destroys or kills? Consider this carefully. Did God destroy them permanently or did he simply put them to sleep, put them in

---

9 - The Youth's Instructor, Nov. 30, 1893

a "spiritual time out" so to speak, until the resurrection? Note Jesus' words –

"Do not be astonished at this; for the hour is coming when all who are in their graves will hear his voice and will come out – those who have done good, to the resurrection of life, and those who have done evil, to the resurrection of condemnation."[10]

All those He "destroyed" in the past He will make alive again; they are not dead but, according to the Bible, are only asleep. God is not a murderer, killer, or executioner! We will study the death of the wicked in detail in another chapter of this book. (It is interesting that the biblical word for "wicked" also can mean "diseased" as well as bad, which reinforces the healing model.)

If God, as taught in the legal model, arbitrarily punishes sinners, then what we need most is pardon to avoid punishment. But if as in the healing model, sin is actually a sickness that produces inevitable suffering and death, then what we really need is healing – we need the Great Physician! It is vital that we come to realize that we have nothing to fear from God regardless of who we are or what we have done. What we do need to fear are the effects

---

10 - John 5:28 NRSV

of a selfish, rebellious heart that resists coming to God for the healing that only He can provide. Only He can give us peace, freedom, joy and eternal life. And those who come to Him He will *"by no means turn away."*[11]

I understand there may still be questions as to the part forgiveness plays in this model. And there's also the questions about God's justice. What role do these things play in the healing model? In the next two chapters we will take a closer look at these two issues to better understand their role in God's healing plan.

---

11 - see John 6:37

Chapter Nine

Forgiveness in the Healing Model

If we confess our sins, he is faithful and just and will forgive us our sins and purify us from all unrighteousness.
1 John 1:9

It is easy to understand the part forgiveness plays in the legal model if one views it as simply an act of pardon. But what is forgiveness really and how does it fit into the healing model? We will address that in this chapter.

There have been many books and articles written and countless sermons preached on forgiveness. After much study on this subject, it seems to me there are two ways of understanding forgiveness. There is man's way and God's way. I will begin with man's way and the Webster's dictionary definition of the word "forgiveness":

(1) To grant pardon.

(2) To grant freedom from penalty; cease to demand penalty or retribution.

(3) To remit, as a debt.

We normally think of two situations where someone may seek forgiveness from another; 1) When one has offended or hurt another person or 2) when one owes some kind of debt to another person.

As a result of these situations, some sort of penalty or payback is usually required. In order for the guilty or obligated party to avoid the penalty or payback, there must be forgiveness or pardon granted by the one offended or the one to whom the debt is owed. Someone once said: *"forgiveness to the injured belongs."* It makes sense to us that the injured party has the exclusive right to grant or refuse forgiveness. In our world, clinging to feelings of animosity and bitterness against those who have offended us is seen as acceptable, even normal.

There is a story told about a man long ago who was bitten by a dog that was found to have rabies. Back in those days they had no vaccine for rabies and to contract this disease was a death sentence. After his examination, the doctor told the man the horrifying news. "Get your affairs in order; it's just a matter of time. We will keep you as comfortable as we can, but there is no cure." The doctor then left the room. The man picked up a piece of paper and started writing. The doctor momentarily re-entered the room and saw the patient writing on this paper. The doctor said, "Well, I see you are writing out your will." "No," the man replied, "I'm not writing my will, I'm writing a list of names of all the people I'm going to bite before I die!"

Though this attitude may be seen as normal for most people, the Christian believer however must ask, Is this right? What do we see in the example of Jesus? We find the answer in the Bible – not in the dictionary.

The biblical Hebrew and Greek words translated *"forgiveness"* – *"forgiven"* – *"forgive,"* all have basically the same definition – (1) To send away or (2) To release; to let go; to set free. Penalty or punishment is not implied in the biblical use of these words. The reason for this may be, as we've discussed previously and can see in Galatians 6:7, that whenever there is an offense there is automatically an inherent penalty. *"A man reaps what he sows."* This basic principle established by God is fundamental and has never failed, nor will it ever fail. It is a fact of life; every deed – every word – every gesture – every action in life on both the physical and spiritual plane has a sure consequence.

A correct understanding of this principle of natural cause and effect is key to perceiving the difference between the legal model and the healing model. God does not need to arbitrarily impose penalties because His laws are all based on this principle of cause and effect; therefore they do not require artificial punishments like imposed laws necessitate.

As previously stated, right actions result in good consequences; wrong actions result in bad consequences in which someone always gets hurt. For example: A man lies on the witness stand and because of that an innocent person is sent to prison. Years later the man who lied repents and recants his testimony and the innocent man is freed. If the person injured in this case forgives his false accuser, does that give him back the freedom he lost during all those long years of suffering in prison? No. Or if a man commits adultery and later feels remorse and asks to be forgiven by his wife and his wife graciously forgives him – does that erase the hurt in the heart of his wife? Of course not.

The damage created by actions that offend and hurt do not disappear when the offended party grants forgiveness; there are unavoidable consequences to our actions. So if forgiveness does not remit or heal the damage done to the offended party, what is the motivation? Why should one who is offended forgive? What reason or incentive is there to forgive?

First, let us back up a little and look at this from both sides of the problem to make more sense out of what true forgiveness is and what it involves.

When there is an offense or debt, we have already noted that there are two parties involved: the offending person and the offended party. There are differing consequences in the mind and emotions of each person depending which side of the offense or debt they are on.

Let's begin with the offended party. As humans most of us realize that one who has been offended feels a sense of loss, a sense that they are owed an apology at the very least, that a debt of some sort has been created that needs to be repaid in some way to fill the emptiness. Some may desire appeasement for the pain that has been incurred. If there is no immediate resolution of this tension most people gravitate toward desires for revenge and want retribution or retaliation to inflict something on the offender that will incur similar feelings of loss and pain as what their victims have experienced.

It may seem initially that there is really no incentive for the offended person to forgive. After all, what benefit is there in forgiving? Why should they let go of their feelings of resentment, their desires to maintain their right to seek revenge? Many are afraid that if they forgive it will send a signal that the offense was not really that bad or that they are now vulnerable to being abused again. Some feel that as long as they stay resentful and angry that somehow their anger will protect them from being taken advantage of all over again.

What we must realize is that unforgiveness – holding onto a grudge and refusing to let go of our desires for revenge – is itself a deadly poison that slowly destroys our own heart as long as we cling to it. It has been said that "unforgiveness is the poison that we swallow hoping the other person will die." In reality, letting go of our rights to collect on emotional debts owed to us is the only way we can become free from the prison of bitterness. No amount of pain we can inflict on those who have hurt us will bring us the peace and satisfaction that we crave so desperately. Only by releasing through forgiveness those who have hurt us can we begin to experience the healing that our own heart must have in order to grow and be free again ourselves.

Jesus said – *"If you have anything against anyone, forgive him, that your Father in heaven may also forgive you your trespasses. But if you do not forgive, neither will your father in heaven forgive your trespasses."*[1]

In other words, if we are cherishing feelings of contempt and bitterness for another and refuse to forgive – will not *"let it go"* – it becomes more hurtful to us than to them and we sin against ourselves. Our hearts are created in such a way that only by letting go of the feelings of offense

---

1   - Mark 11:25 NKJV

we hold against others are we enabled to embrace the reality of the forgiveness that God extends to us. But as long as we retain bitterness and unforgiveness we block our own hearts from being able to embrace forgiveness from God. The problem is not that God is holding a grudge and unwilling to forgive us; rather we inhibit our own ability to believe and embrace it.

Clinging to an unforgiving attitude, allowing a root of bitterness and hatred for others to flourish inside even if we believe someone deserves it, acts like poison to our own spirit and it can eventually destroy us!

"See to it that no one fails to obtain the grace of God; that no root of bitterness springs up and causes trouble, and through it many become defiled."[2]

We must let it go for our own sake! A friend of Clara Barton, founder of the American Red Cross, once reminded her of an especially cruel thing done to her years before. But Miss Barton seemed not to recall it. *"Don't you remember it?"* her friend asked. *"No,"* came the reply, *"I distinctly remember forgetting that."* She made a deliberate choice to let it go – the real meaning of forgiveness.

---

2   - Hebrews 12:15 NRSV

Now let's look at the situation of the offender. An issue that is often overlooked is about what happens in the heart of one who thoughtlessly or willfully hurts or offends another person. What most often is created in their heart is a sense of fear and/or defensiveness. They might go into denial or maybe try to minimize the seriousness of their offense in order to escape the sense of guilt and the feelings of condemnation they experience in their mind. Because they believe the one they have offended will be intent on 'getting even' in some way, they are likely to live in fear and dread not knowing when something bad will happen to them and so they close themselves away from the one they have offended for self-protection.

In short, what is commonly experienced is a reaction of anger, resentment, bitterness and desires for revenge on the part of the offended one while the offender typically feels shame, guilt, condemnation, fear and often tends to become defensive.

Both of these sets of feelings, whether in the offender or in the offended, destroy trust and openness and friendship between the two parties and creates potential for all sorts of other new conflicts.

So how does forgiveness address both of these parties? Viewing this situation apart from the legal model, what purpose or motivation is there for forgiveness?

The unavoidable fact is that offenses and sins erect barriers in relationships. Looking at the effects previously described on each side makes this very clear. These things naturally create a psychological and emotional state within us called guilt or condemnation which blocks us from experiencing a relationship of trust and love with the one we have offended.

Understanding this principle we can begin to see how this works the same way in our relationship with God. Sin, not God, naturally creates a psychological and emotional state within us called guilt or condemnation.[3] But before we look at that, remember the following text –

"'For my thoughts are not your thoughts, neither are your ways my ways,' declares the LORD. 'As the heavens are higher than the earth, so are my ways higher than your ways and my thoughts than your thoughts.'"[4]

We should always keep in mind that God is not like us. His ways and thoughts are more noble, gracious and

---

3   - see John 3:17
4   - Isaiah 55:8,9

righteous than ours. We want to be more and more like Him but we should be careful we don't try to make Him out to be more and more like us. With this in mind let's return to the question at hand. The Bible says in Isaiah –

"Surely the arm of the LORD is not too short to save, nor his ear too dull to hear. But your iniquities have separated you from your God; your sins have hidden his face from you, so that he will not hear."[5]

When you read this, how do you picture God reacting when you sin? Hiding His face from you, refusing to listen to your prayers? But notice the **subject** of this verse. It is not God; God is not the problem here. This verse is not about what God is doing. It is our **sins** causing us to **feel** separated from God and that hides His face from us. And what is it about sin that has the ability to do this? It is the deceptions of sin that lead us to believe God is angry with us, that He will refuse to love us until some score has been settled. It is the same lie that Adam and Eve believed after they sinned in Eden so when God came around they ran away and hid fearing that He was coming to hurt them.

Sin has distorted our views of God so that we believe He feels toward us similar to how we react when

---

5   - Isaiah 59:1-2

we are offended. We are certain, based on our own experiences and our legal view of Him, that He will exact vengeance and punish those who have sinned against Him to appease His wrath. But is this really the truth about God or is it a tragic perverted view of Him designed to keep us away from Him?

Consider the story of the woman brought to Jesus who had been caught in the very act of adultery. How did she expect to be treated? The men who dragged her before Jesus claimed to be representatives of God and she knew what they intended to do to her. But how did Jesus – God in the flesh – treat this woman? Did He reinforce the feelings of shame, condemnation and guilt that she was already feeling? Or did He present a radically different picture of how God feels toward sinners? Take time to meditate on this story carefully in John 8:3-11 and ask yourself what concept of God Jesus was seeking to convey to us there.

Though this woman had intense feelings of fear and condemnation typical of many of us when we have sinned and assume God is offended with us, her feelings in no way resembled the attitude that Jesus demonstrated toward her. Contrary to how the legal model presents God as an offended party needing to be appeased, Jesus' life presented a completely different view of Him. Particularly during the last hours of His life during His trial and crucifixion, Jesus revealed the truth about God and His real attitude toward those who sin against Him. Jesus demonstrated that the heart of God never holds onto an offense, never refuses to forgive and is ever longing for reconciliation and restoration of relationships rather than settling a score.

This kind of forgiveness really means "letting go" of all rights to ever collect on an offense or debt, choosing rather to absorb fully the loss incurred to open a door toward reconciliation. This is what best describes God's attitude toward those who have committed offenses against Him. Because God is love – total, unconditional love – He also forgives without ever holding onto any right to collect on the many debts that are owed to Him, not even for a moment. As you might sense, this is very different from the view of God that the legal model typically presents regarding His attitude toward sinners.

While discussing the legal model in a previous chapter we talked about the idea that some see it as hard for God to forgive and that this explains the reason for the animal sacrifices in the Old Testament and ultimately the sacrifice of God's Son. They assume it was to pay our penalty so that God could then justly forgive sinners.

But think about this: If I owe you a million dollars and come to you and say "I'm sorry, but there is just no way I can repay that money, would you forgive me the debt and write it off?" But before you answer that question, let's suppose a friend comes up to you and says, "I will pay his debt for him." So you take my friend's money and then turn around and say to me, "Your debt is forgiven." But did you actually forgive me or did you just accept payment from someone else and then claimed that you forgave my debt?

If God required that Christ had to die to pay the penalty for our sin, then God did not really forgive us; He just accepted payment for us from Jesus. That is implying that God is not really forgiving at all, that He is unwilling to absorb the loss but rather must be bought off.

Contrary to how the legal view of God has painted Him, God's main focus is to reestablish a relationship of trust with His erring children, not to exact from them a penalty for their offenses. It is not revenge or punishment that God desires but rather restored, healthy relationships with all His children who were created to live in close fellowship with Him. This is clearly stated in the Bible –

*"For if, when we were enemies, **we were reconciled to God** by the death of his Son..."*[6]

*"For Christ also hath once suffered for sins, the just for the unjust, **that he might bring us to God**"*[7]

"All this is from God, who reconciled us to himself through Christ and gave us the ministry of reconciliation: that God was reconciling the world to himself in Christ, not counting men's sins against them. And he has committed to us the message of reconciliation."[8]

Even though God has demonstrated in Christ that we are forgiven from His perspective, there still remains the problem of our fears, guilt, shame and condemnation that keeps distorting our views of Him, keeps us fearful and alienates us from Him.

This is where many of the texts about forgiveness address what needs to happen in the mind and heart of the offending party for effective healing to take place inside of them. And this is where the grace of God is really effective as we see how it applies to this problem.

---

6   - Romans 5:10
7   - 1 Peter 3:18
8   - 2 Corinthians 5:18-19

When we sin we cause unavoidable damage inside our minds and hearts that seriously damages our relationships with those we sin against, whether it be God or other people. This damage is noticed most clearly whenever we encounter a person we have offended. As long as we believe in our heart that the offended one is holding a grudge against us – as we expect they will do – then we will always feel uneasy at best whenever we come into their presence. The closer we get to them the more apprehension we experience as we feel aware of our own emotions of guilt and condemnation because of our offense.

Unless this condition of dis-ease or uneasiness is healed and resolved, the offender will increasingly feel fearful and threatened by the offended party. Without resolving this problem and finding freedom from these feelings of dread, shame and guilt the relationship will never be reconciled. What we really need is peace. In the healing model we can see better that what God values most is a restored relationship with His children, not just pardon for offenses because they broke some set of laws.

What God longs for is for us to allow Him to come inside our minds and hearts to change our views of how He feels about us and cleanse us from all that guilt, shame, fear and condemnation that keeps us afraid of Him. (1 John 1:9)

These intense feelings of fear inside of us prevents us from perceiving the real truth about how He views us and prevents us from trusting Him. And trust, or faith, is essential for healing to take place that can restore us into fellowship with Him. God is waiting to forgive us in the sense of wanting us to allow Him to remove these inner effects produced by our sins that block us from trusting Him.

But it is important to know that this kind of forgiveness has nothing to do with Him changing His mind or His feelings about us; rather it has everything to do with allowing Him to change our minds about Him. This experience allows us to appreciate His amazing love that in turn purifies and empowers our hearts and enables us to be restored into life-receiving fellowship with our Creator.

"There is no fear in love. But perfect love drives out fear, because fear has to do with punishment. The one who fears is not made perfect in love."[9]

You see, when we remain afraid of God, always assuming that He is more interested in punishing our sins than in drawing us into a saving relationship with Him, we will live in fear of impending punishment – the legal view

---

9 - 1 John 4:18

of God. That fear also prevents us from perceiving the truth about Him and embracing His healing love that we need to have in order to be restored and saved.

We can now see more clearly the two sides of the "coin" of forgiveness and that both must be in place before effective reconciliation can take place.

The Bible stresses that *"His mercy is from everlasting to everlasting"* and that *"God never changes."* This means that God always, constantly, compassionately, forgives – God *"lets it go."* The problem is we have been deceived and don't know that! Many are reluctant to come to God because they feel He is angry with them and that He might not forgive them. That is due to the effect that the legal model's picture of God has had on us which can produce a lot of fear as well as discouragement. But God wants us to have full assurance that we are forgiven – He's not counting our sins against us.[10] That's why Jesus cried out from the cross *"Father forgive them"* even though no one had asked for it, no one had confessed, and no one was even at that point repenting!

Jesus is the greatest example of real-time forgiveness that has ever been witnessed. His example of unconditional forgiveness while He was being mistreated,

---

10 - see 2 Corinthians 5:19

abused and shamed is the clearest example we have of what God wants to do through us as we allow Him to transform us into being like Jesus. The author of the Desire of Ages put it this way –

"That prayer of Christ for his enemies embraced the world. It took in every sinner that had lived or should live, from the beginning of the world to the end of time. Upon all rests the guilt of crucifying the Son of God. To all, forgiveness is freely offered."[11]

Love and forgiveness was in God's heart <u>before</u> Christ died! *"God so loved the world that He sent His Son..."* That is His very nature – that's one reason why He died, so we would perceive that truth about Him. When we go to the cross and realize that in spite of our sin God never has and never will feel bitter or resentful towards us, but is only full of compassion and love for you and for me, then we will begin to see Him with new eyes. This reveals the power of redeeming love that draws us toward God. When we begin to realize the intensity and depth of this kind of love, we then understand how it is *"that God's kindness is meant to lead you to repentance."*[12] Our increasing awareness of His incredible kindness melts our heart and

---

11 - Desire of Ages, p. 745
12 - Romans 2:4 NRSV

changes our attitudes which affects the way we live and the way we view God! It is not our repentance that leads God to show us kindness, rather it is God's kindness that inspires us toward repentance! This is what it means to be *"redeemed by the blood of the Lamb"*; this is the kind of redeeming love we sometimes sing about.

Unconditional forgiveness like unconditional love is God's very nature; but we must not let that mislead us into presuming on His grace and continuing in our sins as we mentioned in our discussion on the legal model. You don't change in order to get God to forgive you; you realize God has already forgiven you and you are then transformed by that awareness! This understanding of forgiveness is an essential aspect of the healing model.

To summarize the message of this chapter – God's forgiveness isn't a reward system where if you beg and plead enough God lets you off the hook. No, God has already forgiven us and what we refer to as "being forgiven" is in reality, our coming to accept the reality of His forgiveness that has been there all along. Then as we ask Him to cleanse us from the lies about Him and the negative feelings and misconceptions that sin has produced in our hearts toward Him, He sets us free from our fears, guilt and shame so that we can rest in His love, experience His peace and trust Him even more fully.

Someone may object to this way of looking at God's forgiveness as being too soft, insisting that God is a God of justice! I am sure you have heard many people say, Yes, God is loving, **but** He is also just! What about God's justice? Is it to be understood to resemble what we expect to see in our legal court systems of justice? We will examine that issue in the next chapter.

Chapter Ten

God's Justice

Beloved, do not avenge yourselves, but rather give place to wrath; for it is written, "Vengeance is Mine, I will repay," says the Lord. Therefore "If your enemy is hungry, feed him; If he is thirsty, give him a drink; For in so doing you will heap coals of fire on his head."

Romans 12:19-20

Among preachers today God's grace and mercy are rightly given a lot of emphasis. And have you noticed that we don't hear many "fire and brimstone" sermons anymore? I believe the reason is not so much that hell is an unpopular topic, but that most preachers find it difficult to explain it in a way that makes sense. How can God – whom the Bible says is not just loving, but _is_ love, and who never changes – one day turn and punish those who reject His love and offers of mercy by casting them into a lake of fire where they will, by some accounts, slowly and agonizingly burn forever, or at best, slowly burn to death? In an attempt to reconcile this confusing contradiction, it is often said *"God is not only loving – He is just!"* and leave it at that.

But before we let it go at that, I would like to ask the question – What does that mean? What is God's justice? Are we to believe it is like man's version of justice? Let's take a closer look. In the King James Version of the Bible, the English word "justice" is used only in the Old Testament and is translated from a Hebrew word that simply means – "rightness."

The word *"justice"* is not found in the New Testament at all; instead we find in its place the word *"just"* translated from a Greek word which has the same meaning as the Hebrew, *"righteous or rightness."* Both of these words meaning *"rightness,"* are in some places correctly translated *"right"* or *"righteous,"* but in other places, *"just"* or *"justice,"* which gives them legal overtones thus predisposing them toward the legal model we studied previously.

The problem is that over the years the word *"justice"* has come to mean something very different than *"righteous."* Webster's dictionary gives the word *"justice"* the following two meanings:

(1) Conformity of conduct or practice to the principles of right.

This agrees with the meaning of the biblical word we just discussed. But then it adds the following definition:

(2) Vindictive retribution; merited punishment.

Over the years the first meaning – "to practice the principles of right" has been replaced with the second meaning – "vindictive retribution" or "merited punishment." This is stated in modern dictionaries which are simply explanations of what is defined as 'common usage.'

In most human societies, if one has committed a wrong, in order for justice to be accomplished it is assumed that the offender must receive a punishment equal to the wrong they have committed. If that does not happen people feel justice has not been served. When one person violates another, until the offender *"pays"* the penalty for what they have done it is felt there is *"no closure" – "no justice."*

Many people today are longing to see "justice" done in situations where they have been wronged. But some who have been offended profess to be Christians and because of that feel they dare not avenge themselves. Instead, they count on God to avenge the wrongs others have done to them. These people consider the following one of God's precious promises for them, *"Vengeance is mine, I will repay, saith the Lord."* They are anxious for the day the Lord inflicts on their enemies what they believe they richly deserve!

The word *"vengeance"* in the verse quoted above is from the Greek word "ekdikesis" meaning: "a revenging, vengeance, punishment." Today in the legal view of salvation most people have come to believe "God's justice" is like that. In order for God to be *"just"* they believe He must impose an arbitrary punishment upon those who have sinned in order to force them to pay for their wrongs, and from this belief comes the expression, "God is not only loving – He is just." That expression, like some of the others we have looked at, is not in the Bible. But this following one is –

"For my thoughts are not your thoughts, neither are your ways my ways," declares the LORD. "As the heavens are higher than the earth, so are my ways <u>higher</u> than your ways and my thoughts than your thoughts."[1]

Higher in what way? Likely more noble, more righteous, more merciful and more forgiving than we dare to think. In the Old Testament, God asked Job a revealing question – *"Shall mortal man be more just than God?"* When God says, *"Vengeance is mine; I will repay,"* should we interpret that to mean God would do what we would do? Let's look at that verse in its context.

"Do not repay anyone evil for evil. Be careful to do what is right in the eyes of everybody. If it is possible, as far as it

---

1 - Isaiah 55:8-9

depends on you, live at peace with everyone. Do not take revenge, my friends, but leave room for God's wrath, for it is written: 'It is mine to avenge; I will repay,' says the Lord. On the contrary: 'If your enemy is hungry, feed him; if he is thirsty, give him something to drink. In doing this, you will heap burning coals on his head.' Do not be overcome by evil, but overcome evil with good."[2]

Just what are these *"burning coals"* mentioned here? We find the answer in Song of Solomon –

"Put me like a seal over your heart, like a seal on your arm. For love is as strong as death, jealousy is as severe as Sheol; its flashes are flashes of fire, the very flame of the LORD."[3]

These *"burning coals of fire"* are actually intense love! In this context it is clear that God expects us to overcome evil with good, with love itself. Does God not do the same? But words can be misleading. Many times we need demonstrations. An experience in the life of the apostle Paul gives us an illustration of how God's vengeance works.

---

2   - Romans 12:17-21
3   - Song of Solomon 8:6 NAS95

"At this they covered their ears and, yelling at the top of their voices, they all rushed at him, dragged him out of the city and began to stone him. Meanwhile, the witnesses laid their clothes at the feet of a young man named Saul. While they were stoning him, Stephen prayed, "Lord Jesus, receive my spirit." Then he fell on his knees and cried out, "Lord, do not hold this sin against them." When he had said this, he fell asleep. And Saul was there, giving approval to his death. On that day a great persecution broke out against the church at Jerusalem, and all except the apostles were scattered throughout Judea and Samaria. Godly men buried Stephen and mourned deeply for him. But Saul began to destroy the church. Going from house to house, he dragged off men and women and put them in prison."[4]

How did God bring Paul to "justice"? What did God do to see that Paul got the punishment he so richly deserved? We see the answer a little later in his story.

"Then Saul, still breathing threats and murder against the disciples of the Lord, went to the high priest and asked letters from him to the synagogues of Damascus, so that if he found any who were of the Way, whether men or women, he might bring them bound to Jerusalem. As he journeyed

---

4   - Acts 7:57 – 8:3

he came near Damascus, and suddenly a light shone around him from heaven. Then he fell to the ground, and heard a voice saying to him, 'Saul, Saul, why are you persecuting Me?' And he said, 'Who are You, Lord?' Then the Lord said, 'I am Jesus, whom you are persecuting. It is hard for you to kick against the goads.' So he, trembling and astonished, said, 'Lord, what do You want me to do?' Then the Lord said to him, 'Arise and go into the city, and you will be told what you must do.'"[5]

God converted Saul and later he became one of the apostles! *"My ways are higher than your ways."* God's way of vengeance is not through punishing but rather to convert, reform and reclaim. If we allow God to have His kind of vengeance on our enemy, our enemy very well might be saved! Paul definitely suffered guilt for the things he had done, and he suffered physically as well – beatings, stoning and imprisonments, but he did not suffer those things at God's instigation. God worked the same way in Old Testament times as we see in the story of King Manasseh –

"Manasseh was twelve years old when he became king, and he reigned in Jerusalem fifty-five years. He did evil in the eyes of the LORD, following the detestable practices of the

---

5   - Acts 9:1-6 NKJV

nations the LORD had driven out before the Israelites. He rebuilt the high places his father Hezekiah had demolished; he also erected altars to the Baals and made Asherah poles. He bowed down to all the starry hosts and worshiped them. "[6]

How did God *"get even"* with Manasseh? How did God *"repay"* him for what he had done?

"But Manasseh led Judah and the people of Jerusalem astray, so that they did more evil than the nations the LORD had destroyed before the Israelites. The LORD spoke to Manasseh and his people, but they paid no attention. So the LORD brought against them the army commanders of the king of Assyria, who took Manasseh prisoner, put a hook in his nose, bound him with bronze shackles and took him to Babylon. In his distress he sought the favor of the LORD his God and humbled himself greatly before the God of his fathers. And when he prayed to him, the LORD was moved by his entreaty and listened to his plea; so he brought him back to Jerusalem and to his kingdom. Then Manasseh knew that the LORD is God. Afterward he rebuilt the outer wall of the City of David, west of the Gihon spring in the valley, as far as the

---

6   - 2 Chronicles 33:1-3

entrance of the Fish Gate and encircling the hill of Ophel;
he also made it much higher. He stationed military
commanders in all the fortified cities in Judah. He got rid
of the foreign gods and removed the image from the temple
of the LORD, as well as all the altars he had built on the
temple hill and in Jerusalem; and he threw them out of the
city. Then he restored the altar of the LORD and sacrificed
fellowship offerings and thank offerings on it, and told
Judah to serve the LORD, the God of Israel."[7]

God's way of taking vengeance on Manasseh was the same as with Paul – by helping Manasseh see the error of his ways and bringing him to a place of repentance. And consider the story of the nation of Israel when God brought them out of Egypt with all their complaining and rebellion. What did God do to them? God graciously provided for them everything they needed. Where is the "justice" in that? Later in their history He sent them His Son whom they persecuted and rejected. And what did God do to them then? Unbelievably on the Mount of Olives He wept over them – then He simply released them to reap the results of their own choices. In effect He accepted their insistence for a divorce from Him.

---

7   - 2 Chronicles 33:9-16

The term *"God is not only loving, He is just"* really infers a contradiction. It implies God is not only loving but He is also vengeful. If you wrong Him, He will retaliate and make you pay! It is essential that we come to understand the true biblical meaning of the words *"just"* or *"justice"* which really means *"right"* or *"righteous."* Then if we were to correctly say, *"God is not only loving. He is righteous,"* we would be saying God is loving and He will always do the right thing – and the right thing is the loving thing. This is the true meaning of biblical justice, the true understanding of God's justice! True biblical justice from God's point of view is to bring healing and reconciliation, to set things right again. Throughout the messages of the Old Testament prophets justice was seen as caring for others and was actually an expression of mercy, not something in tension against it. Two examples are:

"Learn to do right! Seek justice, encourage the oppressed. Defend the cause of the fatherless, plead the case of the widow."[8]

And: *"O house of David, this is what the LORD says: 'Administer justice every morning; rescue from the hand of his oppressor the one who has been robbed.'"*[9]

---

8 - Isaiah 1:17

142

The way the prophets saw it, administering justice meant encouraging the oppressed and defending the helpless. God's justice is not in conflict with His mercy but is in reality an expression of it!

"This is what the LORD Almighty says: 'Administer true justice; show mercy and compassion to one another.'"[10]
And: *"Yet the LORD longs to be gracious to you; he rises to show you compassion. For the LORD is a God of justice. Blessed are all who wait for him!"[11]*

To see justice from God's perspective we must understand it as 'setting things right again'. Notice how the prophets relate to us the way Jesus would administer justice when He came to this earth. He would not do it using force or coercion but through compassion and mercy - *"Here is my servant whom I have chosen, the one I love, in whom I delight; I will put my Spirit on him, and he will proclaim justice to the nations.... A bruised reed he will not break, and a smoldering wick he will not snuff out, till he leads justice to victory. In his name the nations will put their hope."[12]*

---

9 - Jeremiah 21:12
10 - Zechariah 7:9
11 - Isaiah 30:18
12 - Matthew 12:18-21

The way Jesus exercised justice was to "lead it to victory" through acts of compassion. Those who were weak like a bruised reed or a smoldering wick He sheltered and protected. Notice how Jesus proclaimed "justice to the nations" –

"The Spirit of the Lord is on me, because he has anointed me to preach good news to the poor. He has sent me to proclaim freedom for the prisoners and recovery of sight for the blind, to release the oppressed, to proclaim the year of the Lord's favor."[13]

Justice from God's viewpoint is restoring things back to what is right, by bringing things back into harmony with who He is and what He is about. God is love and is full of compassion for the lost and the poor. Jesus came to bring about God's justice on this earth, to liberate those who are in bondage, to set things right again and to reveal what God is truly like.

Can threatening talk in the name of justice and vengeance and punishment ever serve any good purpose? The answer is, in certain situations, it might. You may remember a discussion we had in a previous chapter along these lines. There are some who in early stages of their

---

13 - Luke 4:18-19

maturity, like children sometimes only respond to threatening language and it is necessary to use it to help them avoid imminent dangers. God is willing to stoop to meet people where they are, and He will even risk the danger of being misunderstood by sometimes employing threatening language or actions so that people will stop and listen. But when He has their attention He prefers to relate to them through the gentle, still small voice of His sweet Spirit. The wonderful thing is that God loves us enough that He will do everything He can, even risking His own reputation if necessary to reach us so we will stop and reconsider our ways! Let us be careful we don't misunderstand or misinterpret the sometimes frightening or drastic methods God may have used in emergency situations as often observed in the Old Testament.

God wants His children to grow up so He can communicate with them like adults without threatening gestures or language. Yet many still worship and obey God primarily from fear, believing He will angrily destroy all His enemies. After all, they think, He is Almighty God, and He has the ability and the right to do anything He wants to do. But does that mean it is right for Him to do anything He is able to do?

However, a more important question for us is this: Can He be trusted with that kind of infinite power? That is one of the central issues in the great controversy between Christ and Satan. Think about this: in the war between Christ and Satan, victory for God *is not* accomplished by the destruction of His enemies! If it were, the war would have lasted but a second! No, the kind of victory God seeks is *to win* His enemies' love! God is not concerned with getting even and meting out punishments for every offense (man's version of justice); God is concerned with doing what is right and setting everything back right again! (God's meaning of justice). To love – to forgive – to restore peace and harmony, love and compassion is what is right!

If God's children reject Him and refuse His love, does that mean it is right for Him to burn them to death? God is love, and what is the only thing love will do to those who reject it? Beat them up? Burn them up? Never! The only thing true love can do to those who reject it is – give them up, let them go! This will be discussed in more detail in the next chapter.

Chapter Eleven

The Final End of Sin and Sinners

And I saw the dead, great and small, standing before the throne, and books were opened. Another book was opened, which is the book of life. The dead were judged according to what they had done as recorded in the books. The sea gave up the dead that were in it, and death and Hades gave up the dead that were in them, and each person was judged according to what he had done. Then death and Hades were thrown into the lake of fire. The lake of fire is the second death. If anyone's name was not found written in the book of life, he was thrown into the lake of fire.

Revelation 20:12-15

In this chapter we will discuss how the wicked die the second death. In previous chapters we have attempted to explain that God is not the executioner of the wicked but that they die from the destructive effects of sin itself working within them as a deadly disease. The next question that comes to mind for many is – But what about the verse in Revelation that says *"and fire came down from God out of heaven and devoured them?"*

In the study of the Bible and especially the book of Revelation we must be careful to identify what is symbolism. As we look at each new scene we should ask as we read, "Is this literal or symbolic?" Usually if the statement or thing described makes no sense or violates the laws of nature, we should understand it as symbolic or figurative. With that in mind note the following text –

"When the thousand years are over, Satan will be released from his prison and will go out to deceive the nations in the four corners of the earth-- Gog and Magog-- to gather them for battle. In number they are like the sand on the seashore. They marched across the breadth of the earth and surrounded the camp of God's people, the city he loves. But fire came down from heaven and devoured them. And the devil, who deceived them, was thrown into the lake of burning sulfur, where the beast and the false prophet had been thrown. They will be tormented day and night for ever and ever."[1]

According to the rule of interpretation, is this to be taken literally or symbolically? We can understand much of it as literal. However some things are obviously symbolic. Note in one place it says the fire devours them and then in the next sentence it says the fire torments them forever and ever. The fire can't devour them and torment them forever at the same time! It makes no sense, so this part must be figurative.

---

1 - Revelation 20:7-10

These verses, 7 through 10, constitute a summary statement. Then in verses 11 through 15 that follow, John describes another scene that gives us more detail concerning the event he just described in the summary statement in verses 7-10.

After the Holy City comes down from heaven and the wicked are resurrected, Satan once again deceives them and they come and surround the city thus setting the stage for the *"Great White Throne"* judgment described in verses 11-15.

"Then I saw a great white throne and him who was seated on it. Earth and sky fled from his presence, and there was no place for them. And I saw the dead, great and small, standing before the throne, and books were opened. Another book was opened, which is the book of life. The dead were judged according to what they had done as recorded in the books. The sea gave up the dead that were in it, and death and Hades gave up the dead that were in them....."²

This describes the *"second resurrection"* – the resurrection where *"The rest of the dead did not come to life until the*

---

2   - Revelation 20:11-13

149

thousand years were ended" (verse 5) and the final phase of judgment.

Some have asked, why doesn't God just let them be? Why resurrect them again? Does He resurrect them only to judge and punish them in order to see that they get what they deserve? That would seem reasonable in the legal model but not in the healing model. Could it be that God intends to give them another chance to repent?

I believe God will do as He has always done; He is demonstrating in that day something of great significance to the entire universe. This is to be viewed as another vital part of the answers to the Great Controversy over God's true nature and His form of government. Isaiah prophesied that the time would come when *"all mankind,"* every human being, would see the glory of God at the same time.

"And the glory of the LORD will be revealed, and all mankind together will see it. For the mouth of the LORD has spoken."[3]

At the final judgment, all God's creatures, men and angels, who have been involved in the great struggle between Christ and Satan, from the beginning to end, will all be gathered together at the same time and the same

---

3 - Isaiah 40:5

place – here on earth. All of the wicked will be resurrected and stand outside the Holy City while all the righteous are inside. Everyone will be present at this climatic event at the close of this earth's history.

This is the time when *"The glory of the Lord will be revealed."* What is His "glory"? You might remember we discussed this question in a previous chapter. Moses asked the Lord to show him His glory –

"Then Moses said, 'Now show me your glory.' And the LORD said, 'I will cause all my goodness to pass in front of you, and I will proclaim my name, the LORD, in your presence. I will have mercy on whom I will have mercy, and I will have compassion on whom I will have compassion. But,' he said, 'you cannot see my face, for no one may see me and live.' Then the LORD said, 'There is a place near me where you may stand on a rock. When my glory passes by, I will put you in a cleft in the rock and cover you with my hand until I have passed by. Then I will remove my hand and you will see my back; but my face must not be seen.'"[4]

Then we read – *"And he passed in front of Moses, proclaiming, 'The LORD, the LORD, the compassionate and gracious God, slow to anger, abounding in love and*

---

4   - Exodus 33:18-23

faithfulness, maintaining love to thousands, and forgiving wickedness, rebellion and sin....'"[5]

Note here that God's glory has two distinct facets: 1) The glory of His majesty and power that no mortal man can see and survive it – *"Our God is a consuming <u>fire</u>"*[6] and 2) The *"glory"* of His character of love and grace that Moses saw as the Lord passed by. This is the *"glory"* (character) of God that was also revealed in the person of Jesus Christ. The entire universe will see that together at the Great White Throne Judgment. Paul refers to this scene:

"...For we will all stand before God's judgment seat. It is written: 'As surely as I live,' says the Lord, 'every knee will bow before me; every tongue will confess to God.'"[7]

Note *"we will all stand before God's judgment seat."* The difference is, some will be standing outside the city with the wicked, and some will be standing inside the city with Christ. In Philippians he refers to the same event –

"At the name of Jesus every knee should bow, in heaven and on earth and under the earth, and every tongue confess that Jesus Christ is Lord, to the glory of God the Father."[8]

---

5   - Exodus 34:6-7
6   - Hebrews 12:29
7   - Romans 14:10-11

"At the name of Jesus" – in the Greek, "name" is translated from "onoma" which means not only one's title but their character as well. This means that as they see the glorious character of God in Christ so clearly displayed at the Great White Throne Judgment everyone, even the wicked outside the walls, will acknowledge the truth about Him. But those outside the city walls, even though they acknowledge His glory, even though all their excuses to reject Christ have now been stripped away as they witness the love of God for them face to face; seeing it with their own eyes they still remain as unrepentant as before.

The wicked at last come face to face with the enormity of their guilt as they see their wickedness in contrast with His beautiful righteousness (His glory). Their consciences are awakened to the result of their choices in life that have caused them to be outside *"the beloved city,"* and as a result they are plunged into deep despair and inner torment. Jesus describes their anguish –

"There will be weeping there, and gnashing of teeth, when you see Abraham, Isaac and Jacob and all the prophets in the kingdom of God, but you yourselves thrown out."[9]

---

8   - Philippians 2:10-11
9   - Luke 13:28

The wicked will then acknowledge the Lord's righteousness and bow before Him. But as they do, would the Lord have mercy on them if they might even now surrender their heart to Him? Would He give them another chance to be saved? Before you answer this, remember God said, *"I change not."* He is the same *"Yesterday, today, and forever."* The Bible also says *"the steadfast love of the LORD is from everlasting to everlasting."*[10] That means it never ends! So instead of, "Will God give them another chance?" the question should be, "Since the wicked now see the truth about God so clearly will they now surrender their hearts to Him?" Sadly the answer is that even if God gave them another chance they would not take advantage of it. They find it impossible in their hearts to repent because they have destroyed their very ability to do so. Remember, the word repent means to change, to reverse direction. Just as Judas was sorry for betraying Jesus but could not find repentance inside himself, so the wicked find themselves in the same condition. At the Great White Throne Judgment it will become clear that even as the wicked witness everything God has done with their own eyes and are convinced that He has always been completely fair, they still *will not* repent!

---

10 - Psalm 103:17 NRSV

In this way God reveals to the entire universe the ultimate testimony of the results that sin produces in the human psyche. Sin changes people – not in a superficial or legal way, but sin if not reversed or healed changes and hardens the heart against God and His law of unselfish love to the point that there is no ability to recover! They will never change! They can't, they have become incurable! And being incurable they will experience eternal death.

God could artificially prevent their death, but He has said *"he does not leave the guilty unpunished."*[11] He will give them over – release them to *"reap that which they have sown."* But again, remembering that God's ways are higher than ours, just how is He involved in the punishment of those for whom there is no hope? The following is an important principle in understanding God's "punishment."

According to the Bible, punishment, or more accurately termed discipline, by God is only administered as an attempt to produce a *"harvest of righteousness"* in a person. Note the following verse. *"No discipline seems pleasant at the time, but painful. Later on, however, it produces a harvest of righteousness and peace for those who have been trained by it."*[12]

---

11 - Exodus 34:7
12 - Hebrews 12:11

God as a loving father disciplines us to teach us the ways of righteousness. But no good could possibly come from punishing the sinner after it is clear that his heart is so hardened that there is no possibility for repentance or change. That is unless God wanted to send a message to the rest of the universe – *"In the future, you had better obey Me or this is what you'll get too!"*

But that would only elicit an obedience rooted in fear, and God will never settle for that kind of obedience. The Bible says *"perfect love casts out fear, because fear involves torment."*[13] The punishment suffered by the wicked is the natural consequence of <u>what they are</u> rather than some punishment God arbitrarily imposes upon them. Notice what the Bible says about the *"fire"* that destroys Satan – *"Thou hast defiled thy sanctuaries by the multitude of thine iniquities, by the iniquity of thy traffick; therefore will <u>I bring forth a fire from the midst of thee, it shall devour thee</u>, and I will bring thee to ashes upon the earth in the sight of all them that behold thee."*[14]   What kind of fire *"comes forth from the midst"* of a person? Note also the following texts about the cause of the destruction of the wicked.

---

13 -1 John 4:18 NKJV
14 - Ezekiel 28:18 KJV

"He will have no fear of bad news; his heart is steadfast, trusting in the LORD. His heart is secure, he will have no fear; in the end he will look in triumph on his foes. He has scattered abroad his gifts to the poor, his righteousness endures forever; his horn will be lifted high in honor. The wicked man will see and be vexed, he will gnash his teeth and waste away; the longings of the wicked will come to nothing."[15]

"LORD, when Your hand is lifted up, they will not see. But they will see and be ashamed For their envy of people; Yes, the fire of Your enemies shall devour them."[16]

"You conceive chaff, you give birth to straw; your breath (Hebrew "ruwach"- spirit or character), is a fire that consumes you. The peoples will be burned as if to lime; like cut thornbushes they will be set ablaze."[17]

All of these passages speak of a fire that comes from within and takes the life of the individual. It is the "fire" of severe emotional trauma. It is the fiery pain of despair, guilt, and self-condemnation that crushes out the life of the guilty on that fateful day. Since they have not

15 - Psalm 112:7-10
16 - Isaiah 26:11 NKJV
17 - Isaiah 33:11-12

157

confessed their guilt and let Christ bear it for them, they continue to bear it themselves and it will crush them. Biblical scholar E. G. White agrees in writing, *"Calvary alone can reveal the terrible enormity of sin. If we had to bear our own guilt, it would crush us."*[18]

Emotional pain and grief can cause great suffering and even death. The following report is evidence of this fact –

"During the January 17, 1994, Northridge/Los Angeles earth quake, over one hundred Californians literally died of fright. This was the conclusion of Robert Kloner, cardiologist at Good Samaritan hospital in Los Angeles. Apparently a terrorized brain can trigger the release of a mix of chemicals so potent it can cause the heart to contract and never relax again."[19]

Medical scientists have discovered that not only fright, but extreme mental stress can also cause death. Under conditions of extreme stress the body secretes excessive amounts of bodily fluids such as adrenalin which can cause the heart to stop beating resulting in death. This condition is known as the "broken heart syndrome." This

---

18 - Mount of Blessing, p. 116
19 - religionnewstoday.com

is what I believe most of those outside the Holy City on that day will experience.

Again, the lost will die as a result of what they have become, not from something God is imposing on them. It amazes me how men can believe that our gracious, compassionate Heavenly Father would burn His wayward children to death when we as mortal, sinful, selfish men could in no way bring ourselves to do something so horrific as that to our children no matter how wicked they were! No, our God is not a King Nebuchadnezzar who has those who will not worship Him thrown into the fiery furnace to be burned to death![20]

But what about the *"fire that comes down from God out of heaven and devours them?"* This statement is clear and we must deal with it. My response to the question is this: The wicked are already dead when the fire comes down and devours their bodies. Let me give you the evidence for this conclusion. First, the following text from Isaiah describes that same scene – *"And they will go out and look upon the dead bodies of those who rebelled against me; their worm will not die, nor will their fire be quenched, and they will be loathsome to all mankind."*[21]

---

20 - see Daniel 3

21 - Isaiah 66:24

Note it says *"the dead bodies of those who rebelled against me."* The fire is not burning people to death, but simply burning and consuming the bodies of those who are already dead. Jesus spoke in this way of the last day fires –

"If your hand causes you to sin, cut it off. It is better for you to enter life maimed than with two hands to go into hell, where the fire never goes out."[22]

The word "hell" here is translated from the Greek word "gehenna" which refers to the valley of Gehinnon, a place south of Jerusalem that had become a trash dump. That was where the trash and the <u>dead</u> animals and the bodies of dead criminals who had no relatives to bury them were thrown out to be burned. They did not throw people alive into that fire; it was only dead bodies that were thrown into the fire. Yet more evidence is found in the Old Testament sacrificial system. David said in the Psalms –

"For I envied the arrogant when I saw the prosperity of the wicked. They have no struggles; their bodies are healthy and strong. They are free from the burdens common to man; they are not plagued by human ills."[23]

---

22 - Mark 9:43
23 - Psalm 73:3-5

Then a few verses later he said: *"till I entered the sanctuary of God; then I understood their final destiny."* David said he didn't understand the fate of the wicked until he went to the sanctuary. The sacrifices made at the sanctuary prefigured the death of the sinner as well as Christ's death since He died the death of the sinner. When the lamb was placed on the altar to be burned was it alive or dead? It was dead, of course. And by the way, in the sanctuary service, who killed the lamb? Not God, but the sinner. Who killed Christ, the Lamb of God? Sinners!

Note the story of another sacrificial ceremony when King Solomon dedicated the first permanent temple to God:

"When Solomon finished praying, fire came down from heaven and consumed the burnt offering and the sacrifices."[24]

In this passage fire comes down from God out of heaven and devours the dead bodies of those animals on the altar, just as it will come down and consume the dead bodies of the wicked at the Great White Throne Judgment. I believe this is clear evidence to conclude that the wicked will be dead when the *"fire comes down from God out of heaven and devours them."*

---

24 - 2 Chronicles 7:1

There is no question there will be "fire" involved with God's presence in the end when God's glory is revealed. God's presence throughout the Bible is often described as "fire."

"To the Israelites the glory of the LORD looked like a consuming fire on top of the mountain."[25]

"The LORD Almighty will come with thunder and earthquake and great noise, with windstorm and tempest and flames of a devouring fire."[26]

"For our God is a consuming fire."[27]

There are many places throughout Scripture that reveal the truth about God's consuming fire. Upon close examination we can see this is not literal fire like what we are used to seeing here on earth, rather it is something very different. Remember the story in Exodus when God spoke to Moses out of the burning bush in the desert. The bush was burning but it was not consumed! There was certainly fire there and it was because God's presence was there. And although it appeared like normal fire it evidently had very

---

25 - Exodus 24:17
26 - Isaiah 29:6
27 - Hebrews 12:29

different properties than the fire Moses was used to dealing with.

One illustration of the consuming nature of God's fire is found in the story of Nadab and Abihu, the sons of Aaron. It happened at the inauguration of the tent sanctuary in the wilderness soon after the people were delivered from Egypt. Some very important things can be learned from a careful examination of this story. Notice how the story begins.

"Then Aaron lifted his hands toward the people and blessed them. And having sacrificed the sin offering, the burnt offering and the fellowship offering, he stepped down. Moses and Aaron then went into the Tent of Meeting. When they came out, they blessed the people; and the glory of the LORD appeared to all the people. Fire came out from the presence of the LORD and consumed the burnt offering and the fat portions on the altar. And when all the people saw it, they shouted for joy and fell facedown."[28]

Now read what happened immediately following this incredible worship experience and notice how similar the wording is to what we just read –

---

28 - Leviticus 9:22-24

"Aaron's sons Nadab and Abihu took their censers, put fire in them and added incense; and they offered unauthorized fire (the KJV renders it 'strange fire') *before the LORD, contrary to his command. So fire came out from the presence of the LORD and consumed them, and they died before the LORD.*"[29]

The first time fire came out from God's presence it consumed the sacrifices offered for sin. But the second time the exact same wording is used, instead of sacrifices, it consumed the two sinners who from the context apparently had offered *"unauthorized fire before the LORD, contrary to his command."* But did the fire that came out from God burn them up, consuming their bodies? Note what is reported a few verses later – *"So they came and carried them, still in their tunics, outside the camp, as Moses ordered.*"[30] Note the fire did not even burn their tunics, just as it didn't burn the bush Moses saw.

But God's consuming fire that consumes sin and sinners can at the same time be a tremendous blessing and life-sustaining power for the righteous. In Isaiah 33 a question is asked in verse 14 –

---

29 - Leviticus 10:1-2
30 - Leviticus 10:5

"Who of us can dwell with the consuming fire? Who of us can dwell with everlasting burning?" The answer is given in verse 15 – *"He who walks righteously and speaks what is right,"* He *"will see the king in his beauty."* (verse 17) The righteous will thrive in God's fiery presence while the wicked die in it when God at last unveils His full glory. And the *"consuming fire"* will purify the earth of all its pollution as well as *"devour"* the dead bodies of the wicked. Peter speaks of this final consumption –

"But the day of the Lord will come like a thief. The heavens will disappear with a roar; the elements will be destroyed by fire, and the earth and everything in it will be laid bare. Since everything will be destroyed in this way, what kind of people ought you to be? You ought to live holy and godly lives as you look forward to the day of God and speed its coming. That day will bring about the destruction of the heavens by fire, and the elements will melt in the heat. But in keeping with his promise we are looking forward to a new heaven and a new earth, the home of righteousness."[31]

Now the results of the great controversy between Christ and Satan are understood. The universe clearly sees that the wages of sin is death; that it is sin itself that kills

31 - 2 Peter 3:10-13

and that God told the truth when He said – *"when you eat of it you will surely die."* But the sinner does not die the final second death at His gracious hand! Sin itself is the source of death while God is the source of life! God is only the source of freedom, love and every good and perfect gift.

Some claim that teaching that God does not personally destroy the wicked pictures Him as *"passive"* or completely uninvolved or is not affected by the death of the wicked. That could not be farther from the truth. As we look into the face of our Heavenly Father we will not see there the face of a vengeful God who is gratified to see the wicked suffer, finally satisfied that the penalty for His broken law is now being visited upon them. No, we will see the face of a loving, compassionate Father weeping over His lost children as Jesus wept over Jerusalem long ago. The wicked indeed die and they will die a horrible death. The earth will be consumed in fire. Sin and sinners will be no more, and though God's heart is saddened, God's character of righteousness, fairness and love will finally be fully vindicated. "God is not only loving, He is righteous! God IS Love!"

But what will be your feelings as you look out at the wicked from the walls of the New Jerusalem on that day and watch the wicked die in the mass turmoil, confusion and agony that results when God finally unveils His glory and they are consumed by their own guilt and despair? It may be that some of your loved ones are out there. Will you have feelings for them? Will you weep over them? Of course you will. If you are so hard-hearted that the scene doesn't touch you, you won't be found inside the New Jerusalem.

Then at last there will be complete freedom in the universe with everyone doing what is right because it is right, not because they are afraid not to or because they have been artificially "fixed" so they cannot sin. If God was going to "fix" us so we couldn't sin even if we wanted to, we would become mere robots. He could have done that in the beginning without going through this painful process. But robots can't love and God is only interested in a loving universe, not just an obedient universe.

But I believe the most important question for the Christian to ask regarding the destruction of sin and sinners is, "How is God involved?" This is important because, as we discussed in a previous chapter, the internal picture we have of God has a powerful influence over our own character. If we view God as arbitrary, vengeful and severe, we will become like that ourselves! If we believe God is the judge and executioner of the wicked, we will be in danger of taking part in, or at least supporting, the end-time "anti-Christ" system that will persecute and execute those it judges as wicked sinners, *"thinking they are doing God service."[32]*

We should be very careful as to what we teach regarding God's character lest we *"bear false witness of Him"* and distort the true gospel. But on the other hand, if we picture God as gracious, merciful, and righteous as Jesus demonstrated, we will become like that too. Remember, we always become like the God we worship.

As we conclude we return to the symbolism in Revelation, *"Then death and Hades were thrown into the lake of fire. The lake of fire is the second death."[33]* How do you put death and the grave in the lake of fire? You can't. All of this is symbolic language too. Fire consumes, and at last the two enemies of God's people, death and the grave, will be consumed – gone forever. There will not be another resurrection and there will never be any more death! The righteous will reign with Christ in the earth made new eternally! You can be among those who will reign with Christ as the Bible says –

---

32 - John 16:2
33 - Revelation 20:14

"Praise be to the God and Father of our Lord Jesus Christ! In his great mercy he has given us new birth into a living hope through the resurrection of Jesus Christ from the dead, and into an inheritance that can never perish, spoil or fade-- kept in heaven for you."[34]

Kept in heaven for YOU! The table is set and a place is set aside just for you. This promise is real and no one can replace you at this table. If you do not accept God's invitation, there will not only be an empty seat but also an eternal void in God's heart if you are not present. If you have not done so already, begin now making your plans to be there!

Next we will look at the subject that has troubled many Christians for centuries, and that is the subject of perfection. Jesus himself did say, *"Be perfect, therefore, as your heavenly Father is perfect."[35]* Does God really expect His people to be perfect? We will look at this question in the context of the healing model in the next chapter.

---

34 - 1 Peter 1:3
35 - Matthew 5:48

Chapter Twelve

Sinless Perfection or Perfectly Healed?

Be perfect, therefore, as your heavenly Father is perfect.
Matthew 5:48

How many times have you heard someone say "Nobody is perfect"? We all believe that to think of any human being as "perfect" is not realistic, but in Genesis God said to Abraham – *"I am the almighty God; walk before me, and be thou perfect."*[36] And in Deuteronomy God said to Israel, *"Thou shalt be perfect with the Lord thy God."*[37]

Again in Job we find, *"The Lord said unto Satan, hast thou considered my servant Job, that there is none like him in the earth, a perfect and an upright man."*[38] Then 1 Kings speaking of Asa, one of King David's sons, it says – *"Asa's heart was perfect with the Lord all his days."*[39]

As we search the New Testament, we find the words of Jesus, *"Be perfect, therefore, as your heavenly Father is perfect."*[40] Then the Apostle Paul writes, *"Finally,*

---

36 - Genesis 17:1 KJV
37 - Deuteronomy 18:13 KJV
38 - Job 1:8 KJV
39 - 1 Kings 15:14 KJV
40 - Matthew 5:48

brothers... Aim for perfection, listen to my appeal, be of one mind, live in peace...."[41]

If it is impossible for one to be perfect, then why has the Lord commanded it? And since He has clearly given this command shouldn't we take it seriously? Maybe a good question to ask here would be – what did Jesus mean when He said for us to be perfect? Did He mean that we should come to the place where we live a "perfect" life, never committing sin, even by a thought?

Suppose you saw someone who never disobeyed their parents, never cursed, never gambled, never smoked or drank, never stole, never violated the Sabbath, never did anything wrong – would you be looking at a perfect person? You could be in a medical building looking at a well-preserved corpse. A corpse never does anything bad, but they never do anything good either. They just never do anything!

This concept of perfection became rather popular in the early days of the church. In the fourth century, a member of the church in Antioch named Simeon became the number one exponent of this view. Simeon wanted to overcome sin so badly that he built a sixty foot tall pillar

---

41 - 2 Corinthians 13:11

and climbed up on top. Simeon perched up on top of that pillar for thirty years until he died.

Now think of all the bad things you can't do up on top of a sixty-foot pillar. The other members of the church envied him with his perfect life and many of them built pillars for themselves and pretty soon all around the area there were church members perched up on pillars. Simeon founded a whole order in the church known as the "Stylites, the Order of the Pole Sitters."

This was a period when many "would-be saints" began to lock themselves away in monasteries. The idea was to place themselves where it was not possible to do anything wrong. Is this how the saints are going to be found when the Lord comes – perched on pillars or locked in monasteries, no use to anybody but never doing anything wrong? But is perfection simply the absence of doing bad things as many suppose?

Throughout history many have sought the perfect environment where they would not be tempted to do wrong. Which brings up the question – Would a perfect person, living in a perfect environment be insured that one would not sin? That was not enough for Lucifer or for Adam; both were *"perfect,"* sinless beings in a *"perfect,"* sinless environment yet both sinned. Obviously the absence of doing wrong cannot be the correct view of perfection. This is certainly not what Jesus meant when He said we were to be perfect. Another comment from the book The Desire of Ages helps us understand the answer as to what Jesus was saying -

"God's ideal for His children is higher than the highest human thought can reach. 'Be ye therefore perfect, even as your Father which is in heaven is perfect.' This command is a promise."[42]

"This command is a promise." I never thought of it that way! If it is a promise then it is not a demand, it's not something we do on our own, it's something God does in us! And that makes a big difference. In this chapter we will take a closer look at what Jesus meant when he said to be "perfect."

As we begin our search for truth, as usual we go to the original languages to find the definition of the word we are considering, in this case a definition for the word *"perfect."* The Old Testament Hebrew word *"perfect"* is translated from *"tamin"* which means *"whole"* or *"complete."* In the New Testament Greek the word is

---

42 - Desire of Ages, p. 311

translated from – *"telios"* which carries the same meaning, *"whole"* or *"complete."*

Both words mean *"complete"* in the sense of being fully grown, developed and mature; a work that has been completed. So when the Lord said, *"Be perfect, therefore,"* He is saying, *"you are to be grown-up – to be mature – to be complete, whole."*

This is a process that is to begin at conversion, when one is won back to trusting in God. The change here is so great that Jesus said it was like being *"born again"* – *"No one can see the kingdom of God unless he is <u>born again</u>."*[43] In Romans Paul writes that baptism best symbolizes this great change –

"We were therefore buried with him through baptism into death in order that, just as Christ was raised from the dead through the glory of the Father, we too may live a new life."[44]

At this stage the Christian is just a babe, and here is where the whole marvelous procedure of growing and healing begins. God loves His "babes," but He knows it is dangerous for them to stay in that stage of dependency too long. Babies need to grow up and become able to care for

---

43 - John 3:3
44 - Romans 6:4

themselves. Note the following passages that deal with growing up or "perfection."

"In fact, though by this time you ought to be teachers, you need someone to teach you the elementary truths of God's word all over again. You need milk, not solid food! Anyone who lives on milk, being still an infant, is not acquainted with the teaching about righteousness. But solid food is for the mature, who by constant use have trained themselves to distinguish good from evil. Therefore let us leave the elementary teachings about Christ and go on to maturity, not laying again the foundation of repentance from acts that lead to death, and of faith in God, "[45]

"Let us ...go on to maturity." In other words, let us grow up, to no longer be babes but mature adults in the faith.

"It was he who gave some to be apostles, some to be prophets, some to be evangelists, and some to be pastors and teachers, to prepare God's people for works of service, so that the body of Christ may be built up until we all reach unity in the faith and in the knowledge of the Son of God and become mature, attaining to the whole measure of the fullness of Christ. Then we will no longer be infants, tossed

---

45 - Hebrews 5:12 – 6:1

back and forth by the waves, and blown here and there by every wind of teaching and by the cunning and craftiness of men in their deceitful scheming. Instead, speaking the truth in love, we will in all things grow up into him who is the Head, that is, Christ."[46]

This is to be one purpose of the church – to help people grow up to "perfection" or maturity. It is not an arbitrary requirement that we grow up, but rather there are negative consequences if we remain babes. We will not be able to handle well the trials in life if we remain immature. The books of Daniel and Revelation tell us that in these last days we will face a time of trouble, deception and confusion such as the world has never seen. As a church we will not survive that final time of trouble if we are still babes in the truth.

So in mercy God waits for His people to grow up and become settled into the truth. The "latter rain" or outpouring of the Holy Spirit cannot come until God's children have matured to the point they can handle that kind of power. I believe this is a reason for the delay in Christ's coming, because Christ is waiting on His bride to *"make herself ready."*

---

46 - Ephesians 4:11-15

So how do we become mature, or complete? Paul says – *"it is by grace you have been saved"*[47] (remember the Greek word translated saved is "sozo" meaning "made whole" or, to mature, to grow up) <u>*through faith.*</u>" We grow up *"through faith,"* that is, through abiding and trusting in Christ. Remember the principle we discussed back in Chapter two – *"By beholding we are changed into the same image."* <u>We either become like our idols</u> – *"The idols of the nations are silver and gold, made by the hands of men. Those who make them will be like them, and so will all who trust in them,"*[48] <u>or, we become like Jesus</u> – *"And we, who with unveiled faces all reflect the Lord's glory, are being transformed into his likeness with ever-increasing glory, which comes from the Lord, who is the Spirit."*[49]

Again, it is important that we realize that being saved is not an event but a process; a process of maturing and healing that continues until we die or Jesus comes.

Do we want to remain *"babes in Christ"* for the rest of our lives, being blown about by every wind of doctrine and needing someone to take care of us all the time? Or are we willing to grow up and experience a more Christ-like life?

---

47 - Ephesians 2:8
48 - Psalm 135:15, 18
49 - 2 Corinthians 3:18

When we go to the doctor, are we looking for complete recovery? Or do we think, since *"nobody can be perfect"* I just hope to get a little better? Note the words in Hebrews about the extent to which salvation will be completed –

"Therefore he is able to save completely those who come to God through him, because he always lives to intercede for them."[50]

"He is able to save (to heal) *completely."* Because of its preoccupation with being forgiven, the *"legal model"* of salvation falls short of this ideal of being *completely* restored. How sad it is that God's promise of perfection, that is, complete recovery – perfect healing of our sin-sickness, is viewed by many as something impossible to obtain and is thus marginalized or ignored. Perfection has become a subject of much heated debate among some, but after examining the plan of salvation in light of the "healing model" I believe we can see perfection, not as a legal requirement but as a precious promise to those who realize they need God's healing. *"He who began a good work in you will carry it on to completion."*51

---

50 - Hebrews 7:25
51 - Philippians 1:6

Perfection is not a command; and our part is not to heal ourselves; but as Jesus said to the paralytic at the pool, *"Would you like to be made whole?"* As our Physician, God has offered to make us completely whole, completely well, to completely heal all the damage caused by the infection of sin. Our part is to co-operate with Him. People who are willing to do this are safe to save – no matter how much healing or growth may be needed. And we have the assurance that even if our lives are cut short before the healing process is completed, as long as we are continuing to trust in Him, we will be saved. When Jesus comes again He will bring to completion the work He has begun in us! We can then live in a perfect place with perfect people and no longer be a danger to them because we have learned to trust and follow the directions of the Great Physician.

So we conclude with this truth from Jesus Himself – *"Be perfect, therefore."* This is not a command, but a personal and generous offer to each one of us; that if we will fully surrender our hearts to Jesus and place our trust in Him, we will "be perfect," that is, we will "grow up" – we will "be completely healed." As a result we will one day live among the saints and angels in the earth made new! How can we possibly turn down such an offer? I have

179

accepted His offer and what a difference it has made in my life! I will share more about that in the next chapter.

Chapter Thirteen

The Conclusion of the Matter

When Jesus had raised Himself up and saw no one but the woman, He said to her, "Woman, where are those accusers of yours? Has no one condemned you?" She said, "No one, Lord." And Jesus said to her, "Neither do I condemn you; go and sin no more." Then Jesus spoke to them again, saying, "I am the light of the world. He who follows Me shall not walk in darkness, but have the light of life."
John 8:10-12 NKJV

While I have attempted to give the reader of this little book sufficient information to support the truth of the message it contains, it is by no means exhaustive. I have found that once a person grasps the basic revelation of the truth about the character of God and the healing model of salvation, that the Holy Spirit will lead them to more confirmation and a deeper understanding as they continue to study God's Word.

My personal testimony when viewed in the context of the healing model is this: I have been seeing the Great Physician for some time now, and while I am not completely healed there has been great improvement in my overall health, both spiritually and physically, and I owe it all to Him!

As I look back on my life since the time I first accepted Christ I can see there have been many changes. It seems that God has revealed Himself more and more fully to my mind and heart. Little by little over the years, as much as my rebellious attitude would allow Him to, He has succeeded in bringing me to the place where I am today. Not that I do not have a long ways to go – I do; but I also realize that I have come a long way.

The most significant change in my own heart, other than when I first accepted Christ, occurred when I began to see this picture of God and began to sense how good He really is! I then realized it is true; that by beholding Him we really are changed.

Coming to see God in this new light and realizing that He does not condemn but rather saves and heals, and that we have nothing whatsoever to fear from our heavenly Father, has made a tremendous difference in my own character. In the past, even while claiming to be a Christian, teaching a church class and preaching from the pulpit, I used to see those around me whom I considered "sinners" and looked down upon them as unworthy and even condemned them in my mind. I did this because I felt sure that God felt the same way about them as I did. But now I realize how wrong I was. Now I am able to see the "sinner" as God sees him, and now I do not want to condemn or judge. Rather, my heart longs to reach out to them, to help them find the Great Physician who has done so much to help and transform me! Subsequently I have seen the "healing model" view of God have the same transforming effect on others as well.

This understanding of God's gracious character can make the same difference in your life as it has in others. It can bring real peace and joy into your heart. This is the kind of thing that you won't be able to keep silent about. You will feel compelled to share this good news! I believe this picture of God is the true gospel; it is the good news that God is not what His enemies have made Him out to be, but rather God is like Jesus! This picture of God is the everlasting gospel of Revelation 14, the essence of the glory that will illuminate the whole earth spoken of in Revelation 18:1, and is a vital part of the message that the Church must come to value and share before Jesus comes again. John says –

"Dear friends, now we are children of God, and what we will be has not yet been made known. But we know that

when he appears, we shall be like him, for we shall see him as he is."[1]

We shall be like Jesus – and He is like God. If we are to be like Him we must have the true picture of God; otherwise we will reflect a false image of Him. I believe we can find that true picture, not in a legal model but in a model based on healing and trust – the healing model.

My hope is that if this is the first time you have seen this view, that your eyes will be opened more fully to the beauty of Him who is altogether lovely; that you will become more and more like Him as you continue to behold His unfolding beauty and attractions day by day. Or if you already have caught this picture of God in your heart, I pray you will be even more deeply convinced of its truth.

The following comment by E.G. White sums up the message of this book –

"In the vision that came to Isaiah in the temple court, he was given a clear view of the character of the God of Israel. "The high and lofty One that inhabiteth eternity, whose name is Holy," had appeared before him in great majesty; yet the prophet was made to understand the compassionate nature of his Lord. He who dwells "in the

---

1 - 1 John 3:2

high and holy place" dwells "with him also that is of a contrite and humble spirit, to revive the spirit of the humble, and to revive the heart of the contrite ones." Isaiah 57:15. The angel commissioned to touch Isaiah's lips had brought to him the message, "Thine iniquity is taken away, and thy sin purged." Isaiah 6:7. In beholding his God, the prophet, like Saul of Tarsus at the gate of Damascus, had not only been given a view of his own unworthiness; there had come to his humbled heart the assurance of forgiveness, full and free; and he had arisen a changed man. He had seen his Lord. He had caught a glimpse of the loveliness of the divine character. He could testify of the transformation wrought through beholding Infinite Love. Henceforth he was inspired with longing desire to see erring Israel set free from the burden and penalty of sin. "Why should ye be stricken any more?" the prophet inquired. "Come now, and let us reason together, saith the Lord: though your sins be as scarlet, they shall be as white as snow; though they be red like crimson, they shall be as wool." "Wash you, make you clean; put away the evil of your doings from before Mine eyes; cease to do evil; learn to do well." Isaiah 1:5, 18, 16, 17. The God whom they had been claiming to serve, but whose character they had misunderstood, was set before them as the great Healer of spiritual disease. What though the whole head was sick and the whole heart faint? What though from the sole of the foot even unto the crown of the head there was no soundness, but wounds, and bruises, and putrefying sores? He who had been walking frowardly in the way of his heart might find healing by turning to the Lord. "I have seen his ways," the Lord declared, "and will heal him: I will lead him also, and restore comforts unto him. . . . Peace, peace to him that is far off, and to him that is near, saith the Lord; and I will heal him." Isaiah 57:18, 19"[2]

---

2   - Prophets and Kings, p.315

Made in the USA
Lexington, KY
05 September 2019